◆◆◆　本シリーズの特徴と使い方　◆◆◆

JN026128

　本シリーズ（今年度より3年間にわたり刊行予定）では、こ〔　〕上で必要な様々な社会問題への気づきを、スクリプトの助けを〔　〕のリーディングを通して高めていきます。また、単に情報の受〔　〕入れた情報を再編成し、自分の考えを付け加えて発信していく〔　〕で、4技能のバランスの良い英語学習を、段階を追って進めていくことが可能となっています。

　これからの社会では、「他人の靴をはく力」（ability to put yourself in someone's shoes）、つまりエンパシー（empathy）を身につける必要がある、とよくいわれています。他者の行動や経験、感情を（情緒的ではなく）認知的に理解する能力のことといっても良いでしょう。エンパシーは決して生得的な資質ではなく、経験を積みながら身に付けていくものといわれていますが、この力はおいそれとは身に付きません。様々な経験を積み、考え、悩み、その中で自分の意見を形成していく過程を通してのみ、エンパシーは身に付くのです。しかし、「多様な社会で多様な経験を積み」といわれても、なかなかそのような機会が得られないのも我々の現実でしょう。

　そこで本シリーズでは、**Video Watching** のコーナーを中核に据え、ジャンクフードから菜食主義、カーボンニュートラルから伝統の継承、自動運転から字幕の翻訳、気候変動から貧困の問題、そして種の保存から動物との共生まで様々な社会的話題を、北米や欧州以外の視点も取り入れながら提示し、不足しがちな多様な経験の補助となるよう心がけました。また、考えを深め、悩み、自分の意見を形成するために、**Script Reading** では対立する意見を映像で見たり、スクリプトで読んだりできるように題材を選択しました。加えて、**Further Information** のコーナーでは異なる視点も取り入れることができるよう、様々なジャンルの比較的短い英文パッセージを提示していきます（授業時間数にあわせてご利用ください）。

　さらに、英語を学ぶために必須の、(a)インプットとアウトプットのバランス（**Video Watching, Your Opinion**）、(b)語彙の増強と推測能力の向上（**Vocabulary Check 1st/2nd Rounds**）、(c)全体の把握と細部の把握（**For Gist, True or False, Comprehension Check**）、そして (d)情報の再編成（**Retelling the Story**）などにも十分に配慮し、到達目標である自分の意見の表明（**Your Opinion**）にまで、段階的に誘導するように心がけました。

　このような様々な工夫を凝らした本シリーズでの学びを通して、学習者諸氏が、バランスの良い英語力とこれからの社会を生き抜くためのエンパシーの力、そして様々な社会問題への気づきを高めて頂ければ、編著者一同、これにまさる喜びはありません。

　最後になりましたが、本シリーズの編集の労を執ってくださっている（株）松柏社の森有紀子副社長に、心より感謝したいと思います。

2022年初秋　編著者一同

Contents

		Video Watching & Script Reading	**Page**

Artificial Intelligence Helps Make Movies Speak Many Languages

▶▶▶

映画のセリフの吹き替えではどうしても生じてしまう言葉と口の動きのズレ。吹き替え版の映画を観ていて気になることはありませんか？ AIを使ってこれを技術的に解決しようと会社を設立した映画監督がいます。さてその画期的かつ驚きの技術とは？

Scott Mann
Flawless

1 Video Watching for Gist

Watch the video and pick up five keywords. Guess what the main theme (topic/issue) of the video clip is.

2 Vocabulary Check – 1st Round

Match the following words and phrases with correct Japanese meanings.

1. distract ・愕然とする、ぞっとする
2. be appalled ・〜を模倣する
3. sync（＝synchronization） ・〜を修正する
4. simulate ・〜の注意をそらす
5. modify ・（時間的な）一致

Watch the video and fill in the appropriate words in the blanks.

Reporter: How to make a movie work in another language. For decades, there have been only two options; subtitles or dubbing. Many viewers resist watching films with subtitles, which can distract from the action, and dubbing, which replaces a film's
5   dialog.

(Helga Liné (Actor): This is the first time…)

Reporter: Usually (dubbing) results in mouths **1.**_____
     2._____ sync with the words they are supposedly speaking.

10 **Reporter:** When director Scott Mann first saw a foreign language
     3._____ **4.**_____ **5.**_____ film he made…

Scott Mann: I was kind of appalled and devastated because I saw how different it was.

Reporter: … **6.**_____ **7.**_____ **8.**_____ thinking
15   that there might be a technological solution. He co-founded Flawless, a company that uses a kind of visual, artificial intelligence to digitally modify the faces in a film to match the new words.

(Robert De Niro (Actor): Medina and Epic Contest…)

20 **Scott Mann:** The system is taking a very detailed look and an understanding of how a certain character talks. The system's
     9._____ **10.**_____ kind of retime those mouth movements, like subtly alter them, so they fit the new dialog.

Reporter: Flawless uses voice actors who are fluent speakers of the
25　　　 new language. Another company, Deepdub, uses AI to simulate
　　　　 the original actor's voice in the translation.

(Actor: It's not something…)

Oz Krakowski: We need only a sample of 2 to 5 minutes of the actors'
　　　　 voices in order to create what we call a voice model.

30　 **Reporter:** The new technologies promise to accelerate a growing
　　　　 appetite for content across language borders. But in the
　　　　 process, the line between humans and machines continues to
　　　　 blur. Matt Dibble for VOA News, San Francisco.

 Notes

ℓ.2 **subtitles** 「字幕」／ *ℓ*.2 **dubbing** 「（映画・テレビなど）の吹き替えをすること」dubで動詞や
名詞となる。／ *ℓ*.16 **Flawless** AIの視覚技術を利用して映像の吹き替えを行う会社。社名は「完璧な」
の意味。／ *ℓ*.22 **retime** 「（俳優の口の動きを別の台詞に合うよう）再調整する」／ *ℓ*.23 **subtly** 「わ
ずかに」bはsilent letterなので発音しない。／ *ℓ*.26 **Deepdub** AIを利用した吹き替えを行う会社。／
ℓ.29 **Oz Krakowski** Deepdub社のCRO＝Chief Risk Officer「最高リスク管理責任者」／ *ℓ*.34
blur 「（境界などが）ぼやける」

Vocabulary Check – 2nd Round

Choose the appropriate words below to fill in the blanks in the English sentences. Change forms if necessary.

| accelerate | alter | appetite | co-found | devastate |

1. The people in the town were all _____ after the typhoon flooded the area.

2. People are worried that higher oil prices will _____ inflation.

3. She is over 70 but still has an amazing _____ for knowledge, so she is learning three foreign languages.

4. They had to _____ their travel plans because their train was delayed due to the heavy storm.

5. Yahoo was _____ by Jerry Yang and David Filo, graduate students at Stanford University in 1994.

True or False

Read the following statements and indicate whether they are true (T) or not (F) along with the reasons. If you cannot determine T or F from the text, indicate NG (not given).

1. Subtitles in foreign movies may prevent viewers from concentrating on action.
(T / F / NG)

_____

2. To solve the problem of traditional dubbing, both Flawless and Deepdub utilize artificial intelligence technology.
(T / F / NG)

_____

3. Voice actors are worried that the new technologies may take over their jobs in dubbing foreign movies.
(T / F / NG)

_____

Comprehension Check ·······································

Choose the best answer for each question.

1. According to Scott Mann, what is the problem with traditional dubbing?

    a. Voices in the new language and mouth movements do not match.

    b. Actors' voices in the new language are difficult to understand.

    c. Original actors complain about the voices in the new language.

2. What is unique about the dubbing technology Flawless introduced?

    a. It allows audience to select the language they want to listen to.

    b. It matches the tone of voices with that of the original actors.

    c. It changes the actors' mouth movements to match the translation.

3. What does Deepdub use in creating dubbing?

    a. Native-speaking actors of the new language

    b. A few minutes' voice samples of the original actors

    c. A few minutes' visual samples of native-speaking actors

 ## Retelling the Story ·······································

Re-tell the story presented in the video clip, including the following five keywords.

dubbing	mouth movements	AI technology	alter	change

Due to dubbing, movies have been enjoyed in many languages. However, in dubbing, voices and mouth movements do not match. One company introduced AI technology, to alter actors' faces to match the new languages. Another company also uses AI to change the original actors' language to different languages by using their voice samples. Thanks to these technologies, foreign movies will reach a wider audience around the world.

8 ▶ Your Opinion in Writing ·································

What do you think of dubbing technologies introduced by Flowless or Deepdub? Write your opinion with reasons.

I think Deepdub's dubbing technology is great because by using the original actors' voices, their characteristics will be kept. I also believe that young children and people with weak eyesight can enjoy foreign movies because they won't have to read subtitles. However, I prefer to watch foreign films with subtitles. I like foreign films because of their "foreignness". I may not like to hear French actors speaking Japanese on the streets of Paris. I want to enjoy the sounds of different languages. In addition, actors may not want their languages to be altered because language is part of their identity.

9 ▶ Further Information ·························· Audio 03

Read the passage below.

---

https://www.BBC Honors Spirited Away in List of Greatest Foreign Language Films

BBC Honors Spirited Away in List of Greatest Foreign Language Films

BBC's fourth critic-curated[*1] list of best films is taking the spotlight off Hollywood all together to look at the global stage. American-made and English-language films usually dominate the "best of" discourse but foreign media fans know there are 5 plenty of exciting and moving stories to be found, all viewers have to do is turn on the subtitles.

BBC's list scores the opinions of 209 critics from around the globe to create a diverse list of 100 films. The film list represents films from 24 different countries, helmed[*2] by 67 10 different directors, and presented in 19 languages. The largest number of films are in French, followed by 12 in Mandarin[*3],

---

and 11 in Japanese and Italian.

Of the 11 Japanese films included, only one is animated, and that honor goes to Hayao Miyazaki's Academy Award-winning film *Spirited Away*. The critically acclaimed[4] film took the 37th spot on BBC's list. *Spirited Away* held the distinction as the highest-grossing[5] anime film worldwide until it was surpassed by[6] Makoto Shinkai's *Your Name* last year.

15

Notes

[1] **critic-curated**「批評家が精選した」／[2] **helm**「指揮をとる」／[3] **Mandarin**「標準中国語」／[4] **critically acclaimed**「高い評価を得た」／[5] **the highest-grossing**「最高の興行収入を挙げた」／[6] **A is surpassed by B**「BがAを上回る」

Vocabulary Checklist

Check the boxes after reviewing the meanings
of the words listed below.

Unit 1
Artificial Intelligence Helps Make Movies Speak
Many Languages

☐ resist   ☐ alter

☐ distract   ☐ fluent

☐ sync (=synchronization)   ☐ simulate

☐ be appalled   ☐ accelerate

☐ devastate   ☐ appetite

☐ co-found   ☐ blur

☐ modify

Mongolian Youth Seek to Preserve Reindeer-Based Tradition

▶▶▶

モンゴルに住むツァータン族は、トナカイとともに暮らしてきましたが、トナカイの群れは減少し、若者たちも都会での生活を求めています。そんな中、自分たちの文化やツァータン語が消滅することへの危機感を覚え、動き出しているモンゴル人女性がいます。

1 Video Watching for Gist

Watch the video and pick up five keywords. Guess what the main theme (topic/issue) of the video clip is.

2 Vocabulary Check – 1st Round

Match the following words and phrases with correct Japanese meanings.

1. originate from	・母語
2. advocate	・民族固有の
3. native tongue	・貢献
4. indigenous	・〜から来た
5. contribution	・主張する

Video Watching & Script Reading Audio 04

Watch the video and fill in the appropriate words in the blanks.

Reporter: In the northern mountains and deep forest of Mongolia, the last surviving nomadic tribes that raise reindeer can be found. Originating from the border of Russia and Mongolia, the Tsaatan have lived with reindeer for centuries. The Tsaatan people like Karji Marchi and her family depend on reindeer for their **1.**_____ **2.**_____ life, living off only reindeer milk and reindeer meat until recently.

Marchi spoke with VOA but didn't want to appear on camera. She says many young people now are leaving this tribal lifestyle for more convenient city life.

Karji Marchi: Most young people prefer to stay in cities. When they are fresh and leave the first time, they think they will come back. But then they are influenced by other things in the city, and in four years if they can find a man, then they will stay.

Voice of Karji Marchi
Tsaatan Tribe Member

Reporter: The last remaining herd has shrunk to around 600 reindeer, **3.**_____ **4.**_____ about 40 families. Many are worried their culture and language could disappear. But one Mongolian woman is determined to advocate for the Tsaatan language to then to be recorded and taught in schools.

Azjargal Amarsanaa: Although the older generation is still speaking their language, the young generation is 5.＿＿＿＿＿＿＿
25　　　　　　6.＿＿＿＿＿＿＿　7.＿＿＿＿＿＿＿ forgetting their native tongue because they don't learn this language in primary school. There is no curriculum, and they learn English because they will have to depend on it for tourism so they can use it to have a positive future.

30 **Reporter:** Amarsanaa plans to continue advocating for indigenous education rights and so she will continue teaching the Tsaatan children whenever she visits the community as a guide.

Azjargal Amarsanaa: I also want to teach them vocabulary, for example, horse riding instructions 8.＿＿＿＿＿＿＿
35　　　　　　9.＿＿＿＿＿＿＿　10.＿＿＿＿＿＿＿ them. I can then say those words. That's my small contribution to them to teach them English.

40 **Reporter:** For now, many Tsaatan families hope by showing the calm nature of reindeer, more people will be attracted to continue this nomadic way of life. Libby Hogan for VOA
45　　News, Saginaw, Mongolia.

Azjargal Amarsanaa
Tuvan Language Teacher

Notes

ℓ.1 **Mongolia** 「モンゴル国」公用語は国民の95％を占めるモンゴル人が話すモンゴル語。／ℓ.2 **nomadic tribe** 「遊牧民」ここではタイガ（針葉樹林地帯）で暮らす狩猟採集民のトゥバ人を指す。草原地域の遊牧民とは異なる生活習慣を持つ。／ℓ.4 **the Tsaatan** 「ツァータン（族）」(the Tsaatan で民族名を指す。複数形扱い。)もともとロシア・トゥヴァ共和国に居住していたトゥヴァ民族の人々を指す。ツァータンは正式な民族の名前ではなく、モンゴル語で「トナカイを飼う人々」という意味。／ℓ.17 **herd** 「（大きな動物の）群れ」／ℓ.21 **the Tsaatan language** 「ツァータンが話す言語」ここではトゥヴァ語を指す。トゥヴァ語とモンゴル語は言語系統が異なる。

4 ▶ Vocabulary Check – 2nd Round ·····················

Choose the appropriate words below to fill in the blanks in the English sentences. Change forms if necessary.

| attract | be determined | depend | remain | shrink |

1. The country _____ heavily on tourism due to its poor natural resources.

2. Only several thousand snow leopards _____ today because of their habitat loss.

3. Our company's profits _____ from $3.5 million to $1.25 million last year.

4. She _____ to be a professional dancer and practiced for hours every day.

5. What _____ me most to the job was the chance to travel abroad.

5 ▶ True or False ·····························

Read the following statements and indicate whether they are true (T) or not (F) along with the reasons. If you cannot determine T or F from the text, indicate NG (not given).

1. The Tsaatan's lifestyle has changed a lot over hundreds of years. **(T / F / NG)**

_____

2. Once the young Tsaatan leave the tribe, some of them may not come back.

(T / F / NG)

_____

3. The Tsaatan are worried that their language may be lost in the future.

(T / F / NG)

_____

Comprehension Check ···

Choose the best answer for each question.

1. Where did the Tsaatan originally come from?

    a. An area covering parts of Russia and Mongolia

    b. A desert in the southern part of Russia

    c. A grassland in the northern part of Mongolia

2. Why is Amarsanaa working with the Tsaatan children?

    a. To promote tourism in the region

    b. To protect their mother language

    c. To give them chances to leave their tribe

3. According to the Tsaatan, what could attract young people to the nomadic lifestyle?

    a. Their unique culture

    b. Their friendly local people

    c. Their gentle reindeer

 Retelling the Story ·······································

Re-tell the story presented in the video clip, including the following five keywords.

Mongolia   nomadic tribe   the young Tsaatan   city

language and culture

_____

_____

8 ▶ Your Opinion in Writing ·······················

There are only 40 families in the Tsaatan tribe now. What should the younger generation of the Tsaatan do for their future? Write your opinion in at least six sentences.

_____

_____

_____

_____

9 ▶ Further Information ························· Audio 05

Read the passage below.

Efforts Underway to Save Ainu Language and Culture

　　According to the third edition of UNESCO's[*1] Atlas of the World's Languages in Danger, eight languages in Japan are endangered, including various Ryukyuan languages and Hachijo in addition to Ainu. The Ainu language is the only one designated
5　as[*2] being critically endangered, where the "youngest speakers are grandparents and older, and they speak the language partially and infrequently." On a five-level scale with five meaning extinct, this represents level four.

Degree of Endangerment	
Level 1	Vulnerable
Level 2	Definitely endangered
Level 3	Severely endangered
Level 4	Critically endangered
Level 5	Extinct

　　In 2019, the Japanese government passed the law called "the
10 Act Promoting Measures to Achieve a Society in which the Pride of
Ainu People Is Respected*³".

　　This act seeks to increase understanding and respect for
Ainu culture as part of broader understanding and respect for
multiculturalism and coexistence*⁴ with diverse ethnic groups.
15 The government is now supporting efforts to preserve and promote
the speaking of Ainu.

From "Efforts underway to save Ainu language and culture", *The Japan Times*, February 21, 2022（第 1 段落全文、及び第 3 段落の "This act... groups."
が JT 掲載記事からの抜粋箇所、それ以外は弊社編著者による執筆箇所となる）

 Notes

*¹ UNESCO (United Nations Educational, Scientific and Cultural Organization)「国際連合
教育科学文化機関」／ ***² be designated as~**「～に指定されている」／ ***³ the Act Promoting
Measures to Achieve a Society in which the Pride of Ainu People Is Respected**「アイヌ
の人々の誇りが尊重される社会を実現するための施策の推進に関する法律」／ ***⁴ coexistence**「共存」

Vocabulary Checklist

Check the boxes after reviewing the meanings
of the words listed below.

Unit 2
Mongolian Youth Seek to Preserve Reindeer-Based Tradition

☐ tribe

☐ originate from

☐ depend

☐ remain

☐ herd

☐ shrink

☐ be determined

☐ advocate

☐ native tongue

☐ indigenous

☐ contribution

☐ calm

☐ attract

Climate-Driven Heat Waves Increasing Inequality

南アジアの労働人口の約半数を占めるのが建設現場や農場で働く人々です。猛暑の中、屋外で働かなければならないこうした人々には熱中症のリスクがあり、しかしそのリスクを避けるために労働時間を減らせば減給に繋がる事態となります。猛暑は雇用や経済格差を生む環境問題でもあるのです。

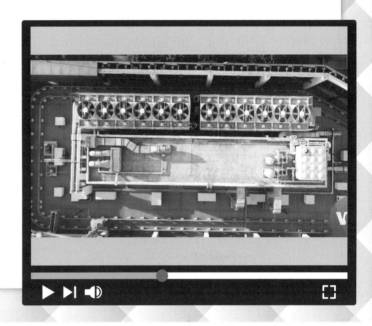

 1 ## Video Watching for Gist

Watch the video and pick up five keywords. Guess what the main theme (topic/issue) of the video clip is.

2 ## Vocabulary Check – 1st Round

Match the following words and phrases with correct Japanese meanings.

1. inequality ・労働人口
2. workforce ・熱中症
3. wage laborers ・不平等
4. heat stroke ・相当するもの
5. equivalent ・日雇い労働者

3 ◆ Video Watching & Script Reading 🔊 Audio 06

Watch the video and fill in the appropriate words in the blanks.

Reporter: The heat has been brutal for construction workers, farm workers, and anyone working outside. That's about half the workforce in South Asia, but **1.**_____ **2.**_____ is not an option for many, like Indian construction worker
5   Kushilal Mandal.

Kushilal Mandal: Even if it's very hot, we still have to work. We won't be able to eat if we don't work. Wage laborers like us work despite the heat.

Reporter: At these temperatures, heat stroke, and even death, are
10   real risks for people working outside. Many worksites shut down early. But that means lost wages. Hours lost to heat are on the rise worldwide. In 2030, a U.N. report says they will add up
15   to the equivalent of 80 million full time jobs.

Kushilal Mandal
Construction Worker

Teevrat Garg: These effects are global, they are pronounced, and they are persistent.

Reporter: Teevrat Garg, an economist at the University of California
20   San Diego, says it doesn't take a full work stoppage to hurt workers' wages. People just can't **3.**_____ **4.**_____ **5.**_____ when it's hot.

Teevrat Garg: It's not about workers feeling icky, or lazy, or just like I don't want to work because it is hot. It's that heat is
25   representing binding constraints on workers' ability to do their job.

Reporter: It's not just outdoor work that suffers in the heat, says World Bank economist, Patrick Behrer.

Patrick Behrer: We think of manufacturing as a thing that occurs

30 inside, but inside doesn't mean protected from heat. It doesn't mean air conditioned.

Reporter: He says heat affects workers even if they're not exerting themselves.

Patrick Behrer: It's harder for you to pay attention. It's harder for you
35 to focus. You **6.**_____ **7.**_____ more easily. And so all of those things feed through to reductions in productivity.

Reporter: And Behrer says there's more on the line than lost wages.

Patrick Behrer: Because you're paying less attention to what you're doing, or you're more tired, you're much more likely to injure
40 yourself.

Reporter: Experts say society will adapt to hotter temperatures. Air conditioning makes a big difference. But that's money companies won't spend on better equipment or hiring more workers, Garg says.

45 **Teevrat Garg:** Adaptation is not free, it is expensive, it's costly, and in general, we find that the poorer you are, the more expensive it is.

Reporter: As the heat rises, Garg says countries will need social safety net programs to lessen the effects on poor people.

Teevrat Garg: When we think about climate investments, we're
50 thinking about seawalls, and we're thinking about green energy, and all of that's quite important. But it's also important to remember that social protection programs and safety nets are gonna play a huge role for **8.**_____ - **9.**_____ **10.**_____-income populations.

55 **Reporter:** Experts say inequality is rising along with temperatures. Steve Baragona VOA News.

📖 **Notes**

Title **climate-driven**「気候変動による」"-driven"は「〜をきっかけとする」という意味の接尾辞。／ *Title* **heat wave**「熱波」／ *ℓ*.1 **brutal**「（天候などが）厳しい」／ *ℓ ℓ*.14–15 **add up to...**「総計…になる」／ *ℓ*.20 **work stoppage**「労働停止」／ *ℓ*.23 **icky**「（べたべたとして）不快な」／ *ℓ*.25 **binding**「拘束力のある」／ *ℓ*.25 **constraint**「制約」／ *ℓ ℓ*.32-33 **exert oneself**「精を出す」／ *ℓ*.36 **feed through to...**「…に影響を与える」／ *ℓ ℓ*.42-43 **that's money...**は that money companies won't spend...の意。強調のため、倒置が起こっている。／ *ℓ*.45 **adaptation**「適応」ここでは暑さに労働環境を適応させること。／ *ℓ*.50 **seawall**「防波堤」／ *ℓ*.55 **along with...**「…と共に」

4 ▶ Vocabulary Check – 2nd Round ········

Choose the appropriate words below to fill in the blanks in the English sentences. Change forms if necessary.

adapt	lessen	manufacture	persistent	pronounce

1. He has a _____ cough because of his smoking habit.

2. Niki started as a small company that _____ running shoes.

3. Peace talks have _____ the tension between the two countries.

4. Children tend to _____ to a new environment more quickly than adults.

5. The judge _____ him guilty and he was sentenced to two years in prison.

5 ▶ True or False ············

Read the following statements and indicate whether they are true (T) or not (F) along with the reasons. If you cannot determine T or F from the text, indicate NG (not given).

1. In South Asia, about half of the working population is engaged in outdoor work.　　　　　　　　　　　　　　　　　　　**(T / F / NG)**

_____

2. When it is very hot in India, wage laborers have to stop working.

(T / F / NG)

_____

3. The cost of coping with rising temperatures appears to have a greater impact on the poor.　　　　　　　　　　　　　**(T / F / NG)**

_____

6 Comprehension Check ·······················

Choose the best answer for each question.

1. What does "80 million" in line 15–16 refer to?

   a. The total number of workers who will lose their jobs in 2030

   b. The total hours of work that will be lost due to heat in 2030

   c. The total amount of money that needs to be invested by 2030

2. Why does heat reduce manufacturing productivity?

   a. Because many employees are absent from work

   b. Because workers find it difficult to concentrate

   c. Because heat lowers the performance of machines

3. What will be most important to reduce the effects of heat on poor people?

   a. Green energy sources

   b. Shelters to avoid heat

   c. Social safety net program

7 Retelling the Story ·······················

Re-tell the story presented in the video clip, including the following five keywords.

`rising temperatures`   `not only outdoor workers`   `heat`   `affect`

`social safety nets`

_____

_____

8 ▸ Your Opinion in Writing ···································

The impact of global warming has become a serious problem worldwide. Japan is no exception. Give examples of such problems and explain what we can do to reduce the impact. Write at least six sentences.

_____

_____

_____

_____

 ## 9 ▸ Further Information ······························ 🔊 Audio 07

Read the passage below.

The Great Wealth Divide[*1]

Asia's middle-class population may be swelling[*2], but the rich-poor divide is still big. The reasons for this inequality are many, but one key culprit[*3] is the lack of inheritance and gift taxes[*4] in most of the region's emerging economies[*5]. The wealth gap is most
5 glaring[*6] in Malaysia. According to the World Bank, the country's richest 10% earn about 20 times more than the poorest 10% on average. In China, Singapore, the Philippines and Thailand, the gulf[*7] is greater than a factor of 10[*8]. A widening rift[*9] between Thailand's poorer villagers and wealthier urbanites[*10] contributed
10 to political instability[*11] that sparked[*12] a military coup[*13] in May.

 Notes

[*1] **divide** ここでは名詞で「差・隔たり」／ [*2] **swell**「増加する」／ [*3] **culprit**「(問題の) 原因」／ [*4] **inheritance and gift taxes**「相続・贈与税」／ [*5] **emerging economy**「新興国」／ [*6] **glaring**「顕著な」／ [*7] **gulf**「隔たり」／ [*8] **a factor of 10**「10倍」／ [*9] **rift**「溝」／ [*10] **urbanities**「都市部の人々」／ [*11] **political instability**「政情不安」／ [*12] **spark**「〜を引き起こす」／ [*13] **military coup**「軍事クーデター」

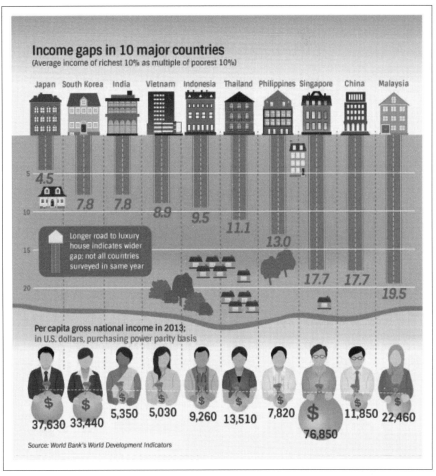

per capita「1人あたりの」／gross national income (GNI)「国民総所得」
© World Bank's World development Indicators

Vocabulary Checklist

Check the boxes after reviewing the meanings
of the words listed below.

Unit 3
Climate-Driven Heat Waves Increasing Inequality

☐ inequality   ☐ persistent

☐ construction   ☐ binding

☐ workforce   ☐ constraint

☐ wage laborer   ☐ manufacture

☐ heat stroke   ☐ exert

☐ on the rise   ☐ adapt

☐ equivalent   ☐ lessen

☐ pronounce

Panda Boom Gives New Hope For Its Survival

中国の成都（せいと／チェンドゥ）
にはジャイアントパンダの繁殖研
究施設があります。パンダを絶滅
から救おうとする科学者たちとパ
ンダの観光客人気にあやかりたい
人々の思惑が交錯しています。

 ## Video Watching for Gist

Watch the video and pick up five keywords. Guess what the main theme (topic/issue) of the video clip is.

 ## Vocabulary Check – 1st Round

Match the following words and phrases with correct Japanese meanings.

1. extinction	・飼育されている
2. species	・絶滅
3. captive	・種
4. overwhelming	・〜を保証する
5. guarantee	・抗えない

25

3 Video Watching & Script Reading 🔊 Audio 08

Watch the video and fill in the appropriate words in the blanks.

Narrator:	She doesn't look like she could save her species from extinction. At two months, Arcee is still a helpless baby. But her birth, along with a clutch of others, has pushed the captive panda population to 300. And that's
5	enough, say scientists, to stop China's national treasure from dying out. Now **1.**_____ **2.**_____ **3.**_____ their nurses to see them into adulthood.
Nurse:	It's like looking after human children. They all have their
10	own personality. Some are outgoing, and some are shy.
Narrator:	They won't stay shy for long. The breeding research base is supposed to prepare the
15	animals for release into the wild, but the pandas' charisma makes them into celebrities. Inside the panda kindergarten we found a group of toddlers eager for human contact.
Narrator:	Seizing upon our television equipment as new toys. ...
20 **Reporter:**	This little fellow is as soft and as cuddly as he looks. But it's also **4.**_____ **5.**_____ the problem, because here in captivity, the pandas get too used to human beings and too used to other
25	pandas. In reality, in the wild, pandas are solitary and sometimes even aggressive animals.
Narrator:	But the temptation for China

30   is overwhelming. Tourists queue up to **6.**_____

7._____ £100 each to hug a panda. In just

under an hour, this one-year-old earns the government

£10,000. For the scientists trying to save the panda,

it's frustrating. Stored at 200 degrees below zero, these

35   sperm samples will guarantee the pandas' future. But

even their most virile donor, 250-pound Kobe, would

never survive in the wild.

Scientist: We won't release one anytime soon because we don't

know how to do it. There hasn't been a single successful

40   example yet. We don't even have experience **8.**_____

9._____ **10.**_____.

Narrator: Science can't help the giant panda back to its native

forest yet. But with this year's baby boom, it has saved

the species. Holly Williams, Sky News, Chengdu,

45   Southwest China.

📖 **Notes**

ℓ.2 **Arcee** パンダの名前／*ℓ*.3 **with a clutch of...**「…の群れと共に」／*ℓ*.13 **research base**「研究拠点」成都ジャイアントパンダ繁殖研究基地を指す。／*ℓ*.17 **toddler**「幼いパンダ」この語は2～4歳ぐらいの幼児の意味。／*ℓ*.19 **seize upon**「～をつかむ」／*ℓ*.20 **little fellow**「小さなやつ」／*ℓ*.20 **cuddly**「抱きしめたくなるぐらいかわいらしい」／*ℓ*.35 **sperm**「精子」／*ℓ*.36 **virile**「生殖能力が高い」／*ℓ*.36 **Kobe** パンダの名前

4 Vocabulary Check – 2nd Round ·······················

Choose the appropriate words below to fill in the blanks in the English sentences. Change forms if necessary.

| breed | die out | queue up | solitary | temptation |

1. Salmon return to the river as adults in order to _____ .

2. She was a _____ kid who preferred reading to playing with her friends.

3. You have to _____ for a long time to ride the new attraction.

4. Dinosaurs _____ around 65 million years ago due to asteroid impact.

5. Selling alcohol at convenience stores is an unnecessary _____ for drivers.

5 True or False ··

Read the following statements and indicate whether they are true (T) or not (F) along with the reasons. If you cannot determine T or F from the text, indicate NG (not given).

1. Each panda has different characters. **(T / F / NG)**

_____

2. Protecting pandas is one of the key issues all over the world. **(T / F / NG)**

_____

3. It is a problem that pandas start fighting each other in captivity. **(T / F / NG)**

_____

6 ▶ Comprehension Check ·····································

Choose the best answer for each question.

1. What is the purpose of the breeding research facility?

    a. To make pandas more attractive

    b. To bring pandas back to nature

    c. To research pandas' daily behavior

2. How do pandas behave in the wild?

    a. They live solely and aggressively

    b. They make many babies to survive

    c. They face difficulties because of urban development

3. Why do scientists say that they will not release pandas into the wild now?

    a. Because wild pandas require strong human support to survive

    b. Because scientists can make better environment for pandas

    c. Because pandas under human protection cannot survive in the wild

7 ▶ Retelling the Story ·····································

Re-tell the story presented in the video clip, including the following five keywords.

| species | extinction | scientist | wild | guarantee |

_____

_____

8 ▶ **Your Opinion in Writing** ·····································

All endangered animals (e.g., pandas) should be protected by people in the future. Do you agree or disagree? Write at least six sentences.

_____

_____

_____

_____

 9 ▶ **Further Information** ······························· Audio 09

Read the passage below.

HABITAT AND ECOLOGY

Giant Pandas have developed to majorly eat bamboo (Schaller et al. 1985). In order to survive, Giant Pandas have to eat a big quantity of bamboo, as much as 12.5 kg in a day (Schaller et al. 1985). Pandas have large chins and use their famous "pseudothumbs[1]" to hold and treat bamboo. In comparison with different herbivores[2], the

5 Panda has very low digestive[3] performance due to the fact that its eating process resembles that of carnivores[4]. The Panda's feeding approach emphasizes volume, requiring it to spend tons of its time on eating (about 14 hours every day).

 Notes

[1] **pseudothumb** 「疑似母指」パンダの前足の種子骨が指状の突起に変化して親指のように見える。通称「パンダの親指」。／ [2] **herbivore** 「草食動物」／ [3] **digestive** 「消化を助ける」／ [4] **carnivore** 「肉食動物」

Lantos Human Rights Prize Winners Vow to Work for Women in Afghanistan

▶▶▶

アフガニスタンではイスラム過激派組織であるタリバンによって女子教育が禁止されています。当たり前の権利を剥奪されているアフガニスタンの少女たち、女性たち。そんな状況下、今回の受賞者の一人 Roya Mahboob はどのような活動をしているのでしょう。

Roya Mahboob
Tech Entrepreneur

1 Video Watching for Gist

Watch the video and pick up five keywords. Guess what the main theme (topic/issue) of the video clip is.

2 Vocabulary Check – 1st Round

Match the following words and phrases with correct Japanese meanings.

1. award	・〜から逃げる
2. entrepreneur	・追い求める
3. flee	・起業家
4. pursue	・規制
5. restriction	・賞

3 ▶ Video Watching & Script Reading 🔊 Audio 10

Watch the video and fill in the appropriate words in the blanks.

Reporter: The award was given to Fawzia Amini, a former Afghan Supreme Court Judge, Roya Mahboob, a tech entrepreneur, and Khalida Popal, an Afghan soccer player. They were world known that their tremendous
5   contribution to empowering and furthering the human rights of Afghan women.

Katrina Lantos Swett: You have a judge. You have a high-tech entrepreneur and an athlete. And each **1.**_____ **2.**_____ **3.**_____, of course, is incredibly
10   brave and in different ways has been a leader for Afghan women.

Reporter: Roya Mahboob, a tech entrepreneur and the co-founder of the Afghan Girls Robotic Team, is urging the **4.**_____ **5.**_____ support girls and woman
15   education in Afghanistan.

Roya Mahboob: Many girls in Afghanistan, ah, still do not have the opportunity to pursue their dreams, as the Taliban banned girls' education. There are 27 million Afghans under 25 in Afghanistan. We cannot ignore their
20   **6.**_____ **7.**_____ education, justice and freedom.

Reporter: With the Taliban returning to power in Afghanistan in August 2021, many Afghan women leaders have fled the country. Some of the women who escaped the Taliban
25   rule in Afghanistan vow to continue working for Afghan women from abroad.

Fawzia Amini: Certainly, we have short- and long-term plans for them inside and outside the country to improve their living condition.

30 **Reporter:** The Taliban have imposed severe restriction on women, 8.＿＿＿＿＿ 9.＿＿＿＿＿ 10.＿＿＿＿＿ to education, work and travel. And just

35 recently, the Taliban announced that women in Afghanistan are required to cover up from

Fawzia Amini

head to toe when going outside of their homes. Sahar Azimi, VOA News, Washington.

📖✏️ **Notes**

ℓ.1 **The award** 米国のラントス（元下院議員名）基金が人権保護に貢献した世界中の人々を対象に、2009年より毎年授与。／*ℓ*.1 **Fawzia Amini** アフガニスタンの女性の権利を保障・改善した判事。／*ℓ*.2 **Supreme Court Judge** 「最高裁判事」役職のため、各単語の冒頭はすべて大文字表記。／*ℓ*.2 **Roya Mahboob** 起業家。アフガニスタンの女性の活躍の場を増やすためにソフトウェア会社を創設。IT企業ではアフガニスタン初の女性CEO。／*ℓ*.3 **Khalida Popal** 元サッカー選手。女性が公共の場でスポーツに参与することがタリバンにより禁じられてきたアフガニスタンで、女子サッカーリーグなどを創設。／*ℓ*.13 **the Afghan Girls Robotic Team** 2017年に創設された、12〜18歳の少女たちのためのロボット制作チーム。別称Afghan Dreamers。／*ℓ*.15 **Afghanistan** 国民の90％以上はイスラム教信者。面積は日本の約1.7倍で、人口は日本の約31％。農業と牧畜への依存度が高い。第2次大戦以降も度々戦闘の舞台と化している。

4 ▶ Vocabulary Check – 2nd Round ··························

Choose the appropriate words below to fill in the blanks in the English sentences. Change forms if necessary.

ban	former	ignore	impose	tremendous

1. Their office has been expanded to double its _____ size.

2. She praised her brother for the _____ support he had given her.

3. Smoking is _____ on campus except a couple of smoking areas.

4. His cell phone rang, but he _____ it so that he could finish his assignment.

5. The government _____ an additional tax on the sale of alcohol.

5 ▶ True or False ·······························

Read the following statements and indicate whether they are true (T) or not (F) along with the reasons. If you cannot determine T or F from the text, indicate NG (not given).

1. Three Afghanistan women received the award based on their activities for women's rights. **(T / F / NG)**

_____

2. Many Afghan girls have few chances to receive enough education due to economic reasons. **(T / F / NG)**

_____

3. Many Afghanistan male leaders also fled the country. **(T / F / NG)**

_____

6 Comprehension Check ··

Choose the best answer for each question.

1. What did Fawzia Amini do?

   a. A judge

   b. An entrepreneur

   c. A soccer player

2. What is 27 million referred to?

   a. Afghan people who could not continue to receive education

   b. Afghan people who are under 25 and need education

   c. Afghan people who enjoyed their rights to education

3. What did the Taliban recently ban Afghan women from?

   a. Working outside of their homes

   b. Travelling abroad with their family

   c. Showing their skin in public

 7 Retelling the Story ·····································

Re-tell the story presented in the video clip, including the following five keywords.

| prize | women's rights | entrepreneur | education | require |

_____

_____

8 ▶ Your Opinion in Writing ·······································

Write your own opinion or impressions about the story in the video clip. Write at least six sentences.

_____

_____

_____

 ## 9 ▶ Further Information ························· 🔊 Audio 11

Read the passage below.

All-Girls Afghan Robotic Team Wins 2nd Place in Intl*¹ Contest

Afghanistan's all-girls robotic team, known as "the Afghan Dreamers," came in second place out of 88 countries in the world competition.

The theme of the competition was for each team to come up with
5   solutions for problems in their society. The robotics team designed an electronic traffic regulator. "We will add counters on the streets and those counters will count the cars that cross the streets. And as streets become more crowded, the duration of the red light will increase and the duration of the green light will be decreased," a member of the
10 team said. After the August 15 political changes, the robotics team left Afghanistan. They are now living and working in Qatar.

Notes

*¹ **Intl** international の略

Translation Agency Advertises for a Fluent Emoji Speaker

▶▶▶

ロンドンの翻訳会社トゥデー・トランスレーションズ（Today Translations）が「絵文字の翻訳者」を募集したと発表しました。絵文字という小さな画像が表現するものをどのような意味に受け取るかは、その人がどのような文化的な背景を持っているかによって違うといいます。

 ## 1 Video Watching for Gist

Watch the video and pick up five keywords. Guess what the main theme (topic/issue) of the video clip is.

 ## 2 Vocabulary Check – 1st Round

Match the following words and phrases with correct Japanese meanings.

1. misinterpretation	·	親指
2. psychology	·	誤解
3. representation	·	心理学
4. depth	·	表現
5. thumb	·	深み

3 Video Watching & Script Reading 🔊 Audio 12

Watch the video and fill in the appropriate words in the blanks.

Reporter: Most do without any problems. But this translation firm think there's room for misinterpretation. So they're looking to hire an emoji translator.

Jurga Žilinskienė: We're looking for somebody who understands
5   anthropology and who understands psychology because emojis are the representation of somebody's emotion and communication.

Reporter: Emojis are essentially just a bit of fun. Might you be adding more depth to them **1.**_____ **2.**_____ exists?

10 **Jurga Žilinskienė:** These little images, as you describe, they could offend people. We need to understand that certain expressions that we probably take for granted will think that it's absolutely normal in the European context. But then **3.**_____ **4.**_____ travel to Latin America or if you travel to the
15   Middle East, the meaning changes.

Reporter: Many use this emoji to indicate waving Hello or goodbye but in China it specifically means to reject a friend. The thumbs up is widely used as a gesture of congratulations, but in some parts of the Middle East, it's taken **5.**_____
20   **6.**_____ **7.**_____ of offense.

Reporter: A client approached the company asking for his personal diaries to be translated into emoji which isn't the easiest to read.

—On-the-Street Interview—

Reporter: OK, so the first one is a London train station.

Interviewee 1: King's Cross.

25 **Interviewee 2:** OK, Elephant and Castle, duh.

Reporter: The next, it's a film.

Interviewee 2: Ah...

Interviewee 3: I wanted to say *The Lion King*...that's a Tiger, by the way.

30 **Reporter:** And the last one is... the last one is just a sentence. Can you give a vague idea 8._____ 9._____ 10._____ it might be?

Interviewee 4: Sleeping... Overslept and missed my plane. Yeah.

Reporter: There we go. Well done. All right.

35 **Reporter:** Next my turn in the hot seat.

Reporter: "Dancing Queen"? That one was easy. Red Bull?

Reporter: Applicants have to take this test, and hundreds already have. It's proving to be a popular job prospect.

 Notes

Title **agency**「代理店、取扱店」／ℓ.2 **room**「余地」物理的な部屋や空間ではないので注意。／ℓ.3 **emoji**「絵文字」bento, tofu 等のように、現在は英単語の一つとなっている。／ℓ.5 **anthropology**「文化人類学」人間を文化・社会の面から実証的に研究する学問。／ℓ.24 **King's Cross** 英国の鉄道の主要駅の1つ。ちなみに、×も＋も、英語では cross という。／ℓ.25 **Elephant and Castle** 英国の鉄道名。ロンドン南東部で急速に変化しつつあるエリアでもある。／ℓ.33 **overslept**「寝坊した」oversleep の過去形。／ℓ.35 **in the hot seat**（くだけて）「不安な立場で」／ℓ.36 **"Dancing Queen"** スウェーデンを代表する4人組ポップグループ ABBA（1972-82, 2021-）の代表曲の一つ。映画『マンマ・ミーア！』などでも使用されている。／ℓ.36 **Red Bull**「レッドブル」エナジードリンクの名称。

39

Vocabulary Check – 2nd Round ·····················

Choose the appropriate words below to fill in the blanks in the English sentences. Change forms if necessary.

| applicant | context | grant | indicate | vague |

1. They took it for _____ that I would attend their wedding ceremony.

2. It is difficult to enjoy jokes without understanding their cultural _____ .

3. The study _____ that over 90% of people are dissatisfied with their salary.

4. She was rather _____ about the reasons why she never finished school.

5. My sister was one of the 50 _____ for the manager's job.

5 True or False ···

Read the following statements and indicate whether they are true (T) or not (F) along with the reasons. If you cannot determine T or F from the text, indicate NG (not given).

1. The company is facing difficulty in finding translators.　　　**(T / F / NG)**

_____

2. The firm wants an emoji translator because misinterpretation of emoji can offend people.　　　**(T / F / NG)**

_____

3. Few people are attracted to the career of an emoji translator.　　**(T / F / NG)**

_____

6 Comprehension Check ·······················

Choose the best answer for each question.

1. What does the reporter say about the emoji's essential role?

    a. It brings enjoyment to people.

    b. It gives depth to communication.

    c. It helps understand text messages.

2. What does the thumbs up indicate in some parts of the Middle East?

    a. Greeting

    b. Offense

    c. Rejection

3. What kind of emoji animal is shown to a man to mean *The Lion King*?

    a. Cheetah

    b. Lion

    c. Tiger

7 Retelling the Story ·······························

Re-tell the story presented in the video clip, including the following five keywords.

| translator | misinterpretation | offend | anthropology and psychology |

| applicant |

_____

_____

8 ◆ Your Opinion in Writing ················

What kind of gestures, emojis, or behaviors do you think we need to be careful of in communicating with people abroad? Write at least six sentences.

---

9 ◆ Further Information ···························· Audio 13

Read the passage below.

 https://www.our-emojis-ourselves-why-activists-want-new-icons-added

Our Emojis, Ourselves:
Why Activists Want New Icons Added

Love them or hate them, emojis are here to stay — and while there are already over 3,500 of them, some see a need for many, many more ahead of World Emoji Day on July 17.

  During this year's Pride Month[*1], Adalberto Robles wasn't
5 at a loss for words — instead, they were at a loss for emojis.

  Robles, 34, a customer service representative from Phoenix, Arizona in the United States had the pride flag[*2] and trans pride flag[*3] emojis available. But what they wanted was a progress[*4] LGBTQ pride flag, a 2018 redesign of the traditional
10 rainbow pride flag with a chevron[*5] symbol with black, brown, pink, white and blue stripes.

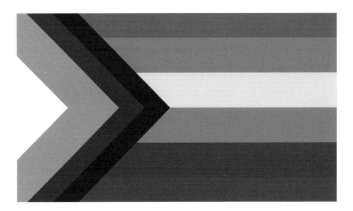

The flag was created by Portland, Oregon-based designer Daniel Quasar as a nod to Black and brown people[6], as well as people who identify as trans.

15　　Robles believes emoji options should be more inclusive, and that the progress flag would be one step in this direction. To that end, Robles has created a Change.org petition to get the emoji added, which has garnered[7] nearly 200 signatures so far.

📖 Notes

[1] **Pride Month**「プライド月間」毎年6月にLGBTQの文化や法的・社会的権利への支持を表明するイベントが世界各国で行われる。／[2] **pride flag** LGBTコミュニティを意味する旗。6色で、いわゆるレインボーフラッグと言われるもの。／[3] **trans pride flag** トランスセクシュアル、トランスジェンダーのための旗。水色、ピンク、白で5本のストライプの旗。／[4] **progress** ここでは形容詞的に使用されている。a new form of (LGBTQ flag) のような意味。／[5] **chevron**「（逆）V字模様、山形紋」発音に注意 [ʃévr(ə)n]。／[6] **brown people**「褐色の肌をした人々」／[7] **garner**「集める」類義語は gather や collect。

Vocabulary Checklist

Check the boxes after reviewing the meanings
of the words listed below.

Unit 4
Panda Boom Gives New Hope For Its Survival

- [ ] species
- [ ] extinction
- [ ] captive
- [ ] die out
- [ ] outgoing

- [ ] breed
- [ ] release into
- [ ] solitary
- [ ] temptation
- [ ] overwhelming

- [ ] queue up
- [ ] store <vt>
- [ ] guarantee

Unit 5
Lantos Human Rights Prize Winners Vow to Work for Women in Afghanistan

- [ ] award
- [ ] former
- [ ] entrepreneur
- [ ] tremendous
- [ ] empower

- [ ] further <vt>
- [ ] brave
- [ ] pursue
- [ ] ban
- [ ] ignore

- [ ] flee
- [ ] impose
- [ ] restriction

Unit 6
Translation Agency Advertises for a Fluent Emoji Speaker

- [ ] misinterpretation
- [ ] psychology
- [ ] representation
- [ ] depth
- [ ] offend

- [ ] grant
- [ ] context
- [ ] indicate
- [ ] reject
- [ ] thumb

- [ ] vague
- [ ] applicant
- [ ] prospect

Water Wheel Picks Up Trash in Baltimore's Waterways

アメリカはメリーランド州にある
ボルチモア港で、川から流れ込ん
でくるゴミを回収する「ゴミ食べ
る水車」が話題です。「2020年に
泳げる港を取り戻そう」をキャッ
チフレーズに始まった清掃プロ
ジェクト。さてこの装置はどんな
仕組みになっているのでしょう。

 Video Watching for Gist ⋯⋯⋯⋯⋯⋯

Watch the video and pick up five keywords. Guess what the main theme (topic/issue) of the video clip is.

 Vocabulary Check – 1st Round ⋯⋯⋯⋯⋯⋯⋯⋯

Match the following words and phrases with correct Japanese meanings.

1. debris	・	（水の）流れ
2. gadget	・	～を取り除く
3. remove	・	装置
4. current	・	行動
5. behavior	・	瓦礫〔がれき〕

3 ▶ Video Watching & Script Reading 🔊 Audio 14

Watch the video and fill in the appropriate words in the blanks.

Reporter: This odd-looking contraption sits on the Jones Falls River that flows into Baltimore's harbor. Every year, storm run-off from city streets carries huge amounts of garbage and debris into the river, polluting the harbor.

5 **Reporter:** Adam Lindquist is with the Waterfront Partnership of Baltimore, the group that sponsored the water wheel.

Adam Lindquist: After a rainstorm, we would get a lot of trash in Baltimore Harbor. Sometimes the trash was so bad it looked like you could walk across the harbor **1.**_____

10 **2.**_____ but trash.

Reporter: Containment booms funnel trash and debris toward the gadget, where a leaf rake pulls it in and onto a moving conveyer that drops the garbage into a dumpster. The dumpster is on a floating dock that can be pulled to shore by boat, where the

15 waste is burned to create electrical energy. The water wheel is more efficient than the way the garbage was **3.**_____ **4.**_____ **5.**_____, using small boats with nets. Daniel Chase, co-designer of the device, says it can remove 45,000 metric tons of garbage each day.

20 **Daniel Chase:** Instead of chasing one or two pieces of trash around at a time, we just stand at the source of it and catch it all **6.**_____ **7.**_____.

Reporter: Chase says the garbage comes from people who throw litter on the ground, instead of putting it into bins.

25 **Daniel Chase:** Plastic bottles, and styrofoam plates and cups.

Reporter: The water wheel uses renewable energy—mostly river current, but when needed, also energy from solar panels.

Daniel Chase: It is run on water, so it's either river current, pushing from underneath or we are pumping water onto it, which then

30 fills buckets to carry the wheel around.

Reporter: The rotation of the water wheel also provides other benefits by putting oxygen back into the river, and thus improving the water quality. Chase says the technology can be used on waterways anywhere in the world. But he thinks

35 that's not the answer in the long run.

Daniel Chase: The real cure is not the water wheel. The real cure is not littering, and the best I can tell, that's done by educating children.

Reporter: Lindquist agrees.

40 **Adam Lindquist:** Our goal is actually to put the water wheel

8.＿＿＿＿＿＿ 9.＿＿＿＿＿＿ 10.＿＿＿＿＿＿. Of course, that'll come through behavior change. If people don't let garbage leave their hands except to go into a receptacle, then we wouldn't need a water wheel.

45 **Reporter:** Lindquist says the water wheel is also helping with another goal—to make the harbor safe for swimming by 2020. Deborah Block, VOA News, Baltimore.

📖 **Notes**

ℓ.1 **odd-looking**「奇妙な外見をした」／ℓ.1 **contraption**「（奇妙な）装置」／ℓ.1 **Jones Falls River**「ジョーンズフォールズ川」都市化、工業化、生態系の回復を経て活用されてきたボルチモアの水路。ℓ.2 **Baltimore**「ボルチモア」アメリカ合衆国のメリーランド州にある同州最大の都市。／ℓ.2 **run-off**「雨水の流出」／ℓ.12 **leaf rake**「熊手」落ち葉掃除などで使われる短い歯を櫛状に並べた箒。／ℓ.13 **dumpster**「大型ゴミ収集用コンテナ」／ℓ.19 **metric ton**「（重量単位である）メートルトン」1メートルトンが1000キログラムに相当。／ℓ.21 **source**「（港のゴミの）発生源」この場合河川から港への入り口を指す。／ℓ.24 **litter**「（ポイ捨てされた）ゴミ」本文ではゴミを意味する表現が多く登場するが、garbageやtrashは一般的なゴミ、wasteは主に産業廃棄物を指す。Cf. ℓ.37 **littering**「（ゴミの）ポイ捨て」／ℓ.25 **styrofoam**「発泡スチロール」／ℓ.43 **receptacle**「（ゴミを入れるための）容器」

4 ▶ Vocabulary Check – 2nd Round ···················

Choose the appropriate words below to fill in the blanks in the English sentences. Change forms if necessary.

| dock | efficient | long run | oxygen | rainstorm |

1. Having conversation is one of the most _____ ways to learn languages.

2. The event has been put off due to heavy _____ .

3. Please wait at the floating _____ which you can see near the park.

4. This goal seems too difficult to achieve even in the _____ .

5. Human cannot live without _____ .

5 ▶ True or False ···

Read the following statements and indicate whether they are true (T) or not (F) along with the reasons. If you cannot determine T or F from the text, indicate NG (not given).

1. The amount of garbage increases slightly after rainstorm in Baltimore.

(T / F / NG)

_____

2. Most of the trash in Baltimore Harbor is litter thrown by people.   **(T / F / NG)**

_____

3. People must join volunteer activities so that they don't have to depend on the water wheel in the future.

(T / F / NG)

_____

Comprehension Check ·······························

Choose the best answer for each question.

1. How is a water wheel in Baltimore's harbor operated?

   a. Using green energy such as water power

   b. Using fossil fuels such as gas or coal

   c. Using manual operation by human

2. What is another benefit of spinning the Baltimore's water wheel other than picking up garbage?

   a. It can improve the quality of drinking water for people in Baltimore.

   b. It can help manufacturing factories near Baltimore's harbor.

   c. It can clean the water by increasing the amount of oxygen.

3. How is the waste being used after collection at shore?

   a. The waste is used to produce local goods.

   b. The waste is used to produce electrical energy.

   c. The waste is used to manufacture new recyclable products.

 Retelling the Story ·····································

Re-tell the story presented in the video clip, including the following five keywords.

| pollution | water wheel | renewable | education | cure |

_____

_____

8 ▶ Your Opinion in Writing ·····································

How should children learn to understand water pollution? Write down your ideas with reasons.

_____

_____

_____

_____

 ## 9 ▶ Further Information ····························· 🔊 Audio 15

Read the passage below.

Japan Deploys[*1] Robots to Tackle Beaches Strewn[*2] with Plastic Waste

---

Plastic trash is a growing problem everywhere, but the volunteers here in the city of Munakata, Fukuoka are exploring a new way to make cleaning it more efficient and less labor intensive[*3]. They, along with researchers, are using a robot designed to do much of
5 the heavy lifting.

The four-wheeled robot developed by BC-Robop[*4], 1.4 meters long and about 200 kg, followed the volunteers as they combed[*5] the beach. They gathered trash in a basket on runners pulled by the robot, which can carry up to 15 kg of waste at a time.

10 The robot can recognize people and automatically follow them as they move around looking for trash. The researchers plan to equip it with a mechanical arm so it can pick up trash on its own.

Notes

*1 **deploy**「〜を配備する」／*2 **strewn**「散らばっている」strewの過去分詞／*3 **less labor intensive**「より労働力の少ない」／*4 **BC-Robop**「ビーチクリーンロボットプロジェクト」／*5 **comb**「くまなく探す」

Vocabulary Checklist

Check the boxes after reviewing the meanings
of the words listed below.

Unit 7
Water Wheel Picks Up Trash in Baltimore's Waterways

☐ run-off   ☐ remove

☐ debris   ☐ renewable

☐ rainstorm   ☐ current

☐ gadget   ☐ oxygen

☐ dock   ☐ long run

☐ efficient   ☐ behavior

Unit 8

Junk Food Advertising Is to Be Banned across All Media Targeted at Children in the UK

多くの時間をインターネット利用に割く子どもたちの肥満防止のため、英国はテレビとオンラインでのジャンクフードの広告の時間制限をする政策を打ち出しました。これに活動家からは「十分効果を発揮するかどうか懐疑的だ」という声もあるといいます。

1 Video Watching for Gist

Watch the video and pick up five keywords. Guess what the main theme (topic/issue) of the video clip is.

2 Vocabulary Check – 1st Round

Match the following words and phrases with correct Japanese meanings.

1. consume	・イライラする
2. get rid of	・好み
3. irritating	・消費する
4. obesity	・捨てる
5. preference	・肥満

53

3 Video Watching & Script Reading 🔊 Audio 16

Watch the video and fill in the appropriate words in the blanks.

Reporter: Children are online an average of 15 hours a week. That's more time than they spend watching television. But while advertisers cannot target young TV viewers with products like fast food and fizzy drinks, they can

5   online. It's an anomaly that will end next year. But do youngsters actually pay any attention to the pop-up adverts anyway?

Student 1: It is really irritating when you, when you're in the middle of a game and you're trying to get on to the next level or

10   that the ads keep popping up and then they make you wait before you can get rid of the adverts. You just sit there and then you get bored. And so you **1.**_____ **2.**_____ **3.**_____ the app and think I'm not going to wait for the adverts to go away.

15 **Student 2:** I don't want **4.**_____ **5.**_____ **6.**_____ these apps and they're things I never want to have. I'm not craving them at that time, so I just click the cross as soon as possible.

Student 3: For me, it doesn't really make that much of a difference.

20   I would just ignore it. So for it to not be there, it wouldn't make that much of a difference for me.

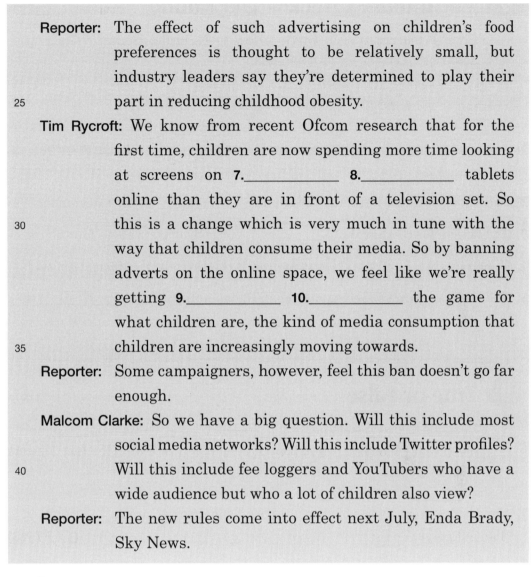

Reporter: The effect of such advertising on children's food preferences is thought to be relatively small, but industry leaders say they're determined to play their part in reducing childhood obesity.

Tim Rycroft: We know from recent Ofcom research that for the first time, children are now spending more time looking at screens on **7._____** **8._____** tablets online than they are in front of a television set. So this is a change which is very much in tune with the way that children consume their media. So by banning adverts on the online space, we feel like we're really getting **9._____** **10._____** the game for what children are, the kind of media consumption that children are increasingly moving towards.

Reporter: Some campaigners, however, feel this ban doesn't go far enough.

Malcom Clarke: So we have a big question. Will this include most social media networks? Will this include Twitter profiles? Will this include fee loggers and YouTubers who have a wide audience but who a lot of children also view?

Reporter: The new rules come into effect next July, Enda Brady, Sky News.

📖✏️ **Notes**

ℓ.4 **fizzy** 「発泡（炭酸）性の」／*ℓ.5* **anomaly** 「異常（なこと）」／*ℓ.7* **adverts** advertisement の略。ad と略されることもある。／*ℓ.13* **app** 「アプリ」application の略。／*ℓ.14* **go away** 「消える、なくなる」／*ℓ.17* **craving** crave「切望する」の進行形。／*ℓ.26* **Ofcom** 英国において電気通信・放送などの監督を行なう規制機関。2003年創設。／*ℓ.30* **in tune with~** 「~と一致して」反意は out of tune with。／*ℓ.36* **campaigner** 「（社会的、政治的な活動をする）運動家」／*ℓ.39* **Twitter profile** Twitter ユーザーが自己紹介をできる部分。プロフィール画像のほか、名前、肩書き、場所、ホームページなどを登録できる。／*ℓ.42* **come into effect** 「（法律・制度などが）施行される、発行する」go into effect とも言える。／*ℓ.42* **next July** 「2017年7月」

Vocabulary Check – 2nd Round ··················

Choose the appropriate words below to fill in the blanks in the English sentences. Change forms if necessary.

attention	industry	effect	product	relatively

1. You must be careful of ordering at a restaurant if you are allergic to certain _____.

2. She sat down at her desk and turned her _____ to her assignment.

3. The direction says that the _____ of the drug lasts about four hours.

4. Tomatoes are _____ easy to grow if they are given sufficient space.

5. The last ten years has seen a decline in the manufacturing _____.

5 **True or False** ···

Read the following statements and indicate whether they are true (T) or not (F) along with the reason. If you cannot determine T or F from the text, indicate NG (not given).

1. Children can see adverts of unhealthy food and drinks more on TV than online. **(T / F / NG)**

_____

2. The ban is set because the adverts give big influence on children's choice of food. **(T / F / NG)**

_____

3. Some people think the extent of the ban is questionable. **(T / F / NG)**

_____

56

6 Comprehension Check ·····················

Choose the best answer for each question.

1. When does the first student interviewed get annoyed?

    a. When adverts disturb her from playing the game

    b. When interesting adverts finish so quickly

    c. When the same adverts keep appearing

2. What does the industry leader say on the setting of the ban?

    a. It alters the way children consume fast food.

    b. It corresponds with the children's tendency of using media.

    c. It guides children to judge what they see by themselves.

3. What is the campaigner's opinion?

    a. The ban may not cover all of the social media networks.

    b. Twitter profiles may hide something children should watch.

    c. We should encourage more children to watch YouTube.

7 Retelling the Story ·····················

Re-tell the story presented in the video clip, including the following five keywords.

| target | advertising | relatively small | food industries | protect |

_____

_____

8 Your Opinion in Writing ·····································

Do you think that the ban on online advertisements of unhealthy foods and drink is effective to protect children from getting obese? Why or why not? Write at least six sentences.

_____

_____

_____

_____

Further Information ···························· 🔊 **Audio 17**

Read the passage and the checklist below.

Essential Standards Checklist

The Essential Standards Checklist presents the recommended interventions*¹ necessary for a successful school-based obesity prevention strategy focused on school-age children and adolescents. The checklist assesses the application*² of the recommended
5 interventions and is useful for countries to use at a national level to determine their programmatic strengths and weaknesses and to develop a prioritized action plan to revise their obesity strategy for school-age children and adolescents.

Interventions to Prevent Obesity Through the Community Environment			Yes	No
Restrictions on Advertising of Foods and Beverages to School-Age Children				
26. *³		Are restrictions in place on the advertising of foods and beverages to school-age children and or adolescents?	☐	☐
		If yes, are these restrictions monitored regularly and what enforcement measures*⁴ are used for violators of the restrictions?	☐	☐
27.		Has an assessment of child and adolescent exposure to marketing of unhealthy foods and beverages been conducted?	☐	☐
28.		Has advocacy*⁵ with consumer interest groups or other organizations been conducted to measure child and adolescent exposure to marketing of unhealthy foods and monitor adherence to*⁶ restrictions?	☐	☐
29.		Is advocacy currently in place for the implementation*⁷ of restrictions on the advertising of foods and beverages to school-age children and adolescents?	☐	☐

 Notes

*¹ **the recommended interventions** UNICEF が提案している指導内容を指す。指導内容の詳細は、https://unicefeaproinasactoolkit.wordpress.com/inasac-toolkit/ の Section C に掲載されている。／ *² **application**「利用、適用」／ *³ ここでは項目26からスタートしているが、これより前に学校での取り組みなど別の観点に関するチェックリスト１～25が掲載されている。／ *⁴ **enforcement measure**「施行措置」／ *⁵ **advocacy**「支援、擁護」／ *⁶ **adherence to**「～への順守」／ *⁷ **implementation**「実施、推進」

Vocabulary Checklist

Check the boxes after reviewing the meanings
of the words listed below.

Unit 8
Junk Food Advertising Is to Be Banned across All Media Targeted at Children in the UK

☐ industry

☐ product

☐ attention

☐ irritating

☐ get rid of

☐ effect

☐ preference

☐ relatively

☐ obesity

☐ in tune with

☐ consume

Technology Helps Find One of the World's Most Sought-After Shipwrecks

▶▶▶

2022年3月、アーネスト・シャクルトンが率いた伝説のエンデュアランス号がウェッデル海の海底で、なんと1世紀以上を経て発見されたという驚きのニュースが飛び込んできました。いったいどのような技術の進歩によってこの発見が実現したのでしょう。

 1 ## Video Watching for Gist ······

Watch the video and pick up five keywords. Guess what the main theme (topic/issue) of the video clip is.

 2 ## Vocabulary Check – 1st Round ·········

Match the following words and phrases with correct Japanese meanings.

1. state-of-the-art	・海底
2. satellite imagery	・最新鋭の
3. locate	・衛星画像
4. seabed	・〜を感知する
5. detect	・〜の位置を特定する

61

3 Video Watching & Script Reading 🔊 Audio 18

Watch the video and fill in the appropriate words in the blanks.

Reporter: An expedition led by polar geographer John Shears recently discovered the Endurance, the last ship of famed British explorer Ernest Shackleton, on the floor of the Weddell Sea of Antarctica.

5 **John Shears:** Technology was the reason that we found the wreck this time.

Reporter: Starting with a state-of-the-art ship that **1.**_____ **2.**_____ **3.**_____ thick ice, and satellite imagery that help locate the general area where in 1915, Shackleton

10 and his 27-member crew last saw the ship disappear into the ice. They left on lifeboats and all survived.

John Shears: Having radar satellite imagery was very important to us, so we knew exactly what the sea ice was doing and we could pulse

15 our direction and route through the sea ice.

Reporter: Humans cannot dive safely in the area, so the team sent an underwater robot

20 to scan the seabed using sonar to look for anomalies. The team tethered the robot to the boat

25 **4.**_____ **5.**_____ its loss.

Nico Vincent: As we were connected by a wire, we got a real-time data, feedback on the surface. And so you have cameras and you see what the vehicle is seeing.

Reporter: When the sonar detected something, it would send

30　an alert to the team above, who would activate the robot's lights and cameras. This is how they got their first glimpse of the Endurance. Many believe the Endurance discovery is the most significant find since the discovery of the Titanic nearly 40 years ago, and has now opened up a 6.＿＿＿＿＿＿

35　　**7.**＿＿＿＿＿＿ opportunities.

Donald Lamont: The potential for 3D models are holographic representations, even for a replica ship.

Reporter: Shackleton died 100 years ago in the Antarctic **8.**＿＿＿＿＿＿ **9.**＿＿＿＿＿＿ **10.**＿＿＿＿＿＿ expedition.

40　Thanks to technology, his Endurance will be brought back to life to educate and inspire the world. Julie Taboh, VOA News.

📖 Notes

Title **sought-after**「（入手が）困難な」ここでは「捜すのが困難な」の意。／*Title* **shipwreck**「沈没船」／*ℓ*.1 **polar geographer**「極地地理学者」／*ℓ*.2 **Endurance**「エンデュランス号」シャクルトンの船の名前。「忍耐」の意味。／*ℓ*.3 **Ernest Shackleton** 南極探検家（1874-1922）。彼の活躍は『そして、奇跡は起こった！―シャクルトン隊、全員生還』（評論社）に詳しい。／*ℓ ℓ*.3-4 **the Weddell Sea**「ウェッデル海」大西洋南端、南極大陸への湾入部の海域。／*ℓ*.5 **wreck** 難破船／*ℓ ℓ*.14-15 **pulse our direction and route**「（パルス信号を発して）方角と航路を検知する」／*ℓ*.21 **sonar**「音波探知機」Sound Navigation and Ranging の略。／*ℓ*.22 **anomaly** ⇨ Unit 8 p. 55 参照／*ℓ*.33 **find** ここでは名詞で「発見」の意味。／*ℓ ℓ*.36-37 **holographic representation**「ホログラフィックな（3次元像を記録・再生する技術を用いた）描写」

4 ▶ Vocabulary Check – 2nd Round ·····················

Choose the appropriate words below to fill in the blanks in the English sentences. Change forms if necessary.

| an expedition | get a glimpse of | inspire | significant | tether |

1. The speech Steve Jobs made at Stanford University in 2005 _____ many young people around the world.

2. The fans crowded around the door to _____ athletes leaving the stadium.

3. A group of scientists went on _____ to the Amazon rainforest to explore tropical plants.

4. He _____ his horse to the tree yesterday, but somehow it escaped.

5. He made a _____ contribution to the field of cancer research.

5 ▶ True or False ···

Read the following statements and indicate whether they are true (T) or not (F) along with the reasons. If you cannot determine T or F from the text, indicate NG (not given).

1. John Shears was a famous explorer who led the ship Endurance more than a hundred years ago. **(T / F / NG)**

_____

2. Without the latest technology, the discovery of the Endurance would not have been possible. **(T / F / NG)**

_____

3. The discovery of the Endurance is considered the most important discovery of the century. **(T / F / NG)**

_____

6 Comprehension Check ·····································

Choose the best answer for each question.

1. What helped identify the area where the Endurance sank?

    a. Underwater cameras

    b. Professional divers

    c. Satellite imagery

2. What technology was used to find the wrecked ship on the seabed?

    a. A drone observing above the area

    b. An underwater robot and sonar

    c. A holographic model of the ship

3. How was the team on the surface notified of the detection of the underwater wreck?

    a. An alert went off.

    b. A tether was pulled

    c. A flashlight was turned on

7 Retelling the Story ·······································

Re-tell the story presented in the video clip, including the following five keywords.

| discover | the Endurance | a satellite | an underwater robot |

| significant |

_____

_____

8 ▶ Your Opinion in Writing ·····························

Technologies have been used to educate the public about the value of cultural heritages. Have you seen or heard of examples? Write at least six sentences.

_____

_____

_____

_____

9 ▶ Further Information ····························· Audio 19

Read the passage below.

https://www.rebuilding-notre-dame-under-a-3d-bim-model

Rebuilding Notre-Dam under a 3D*1 BIM*2 Model

After the tragic fire that destroyed part of the French cathedral of Notre Dame in Paris, its reconstruction*3 began. The fire, which started on the roof of the infrastructure*4, consumed 1,000-year-old oak beams*5 bringing down its 19th-
5 century spire and releasing tons of molten lead*6 on the stone vaults*7.

In the reconstruction process, which started two years ago, digital models and innovative tools have taken a great part of the limelight*8. The U.S. software company Autodesk
10 Inc.*9 reacted immediately by offering its resources for the reconstruction of the cathedral. They began to work on a 3D BIM model a few weeks later that would, in turn, help create

a historical digital record to increase resilience[*10] in future events.

French Army General[*11] Jean-Louis Georgelin, in charge of supervision[*12], emphasized that "the use of digital technologies was essential for the public institution[*13]." He added that "the use of cutting-edge[*14] design and construction and BIM technologies are leveraged[*15] to help prepare for the reopening of the cathedral."

Notes

[*1] **3D** three-dimensional の略。／[*2] **BIM** Building Information Modeling の略。コンピュータ上に3次元のデジタルモデルを構築する技術。／[*3] **reconstruction**「再建」／[*4] **infrastructure**「構造基盤」／[*5] **oak beam**「オーク材の梁（はり）」／[*6] **molten lead**「溶融鉛・溶けた鉛」／[*7] **vault**「アーチ型の天井・丸天井」／[*8] **the limelight**「注目の的」／[*9] **Autodesk Inc.**「オートデスク社」Inc. は Incorporated の略。／[*10] **resilience**「耐性」／[*11] **Army General**「陸軍将軍・元軍統合参謀総長」／[*12] **in charge of supervision**「監督を担当した」／[*13] **public institution**「公共施設」／[*14] **cutting-edge**「最先端の」／[*15] **leverage**「〜を活用する」

Vocabulary Checklist

Check the boxes after reviewing the meanings
of the words listed below.

Unit 9
Technology Helps Find One of the World's Most Sought-After Shipwrecks

☐ an expedition   ☐ detect

☐ state-of-the-art   ☐ activate

☐ satellite imagery   ☐ get a glimpse of

☐ locate   ☐ significant

☐ seabed   ☐ open up

☐ tether   ☐ inspire

Self-Driving Trucks May Beat Autonomous Cars in Race for Acceptance

物流の需要の高さと運転手のなり手不足というプレッシャーを抱える輸送業界にとって、運転席に誰もいない自動運転トラックの開発はその大きな打開策の一つとなり得るでしょう。しかし、アメリカで300万人以上いるトラック運転手の職に影響はないのでしょうか。

Yielding to another vehicle on surface street

 1 **Video Watching for Gist**

Watch the video and pick up five keywords. Guess what the main theme (topic/issue) of the video clip is.

2 **Vocabulary Check – 1st Round**

Match the following words and phrases with correct Japanese meanings.

1. autonomous car	・承認
2. momentum	・自律走行車
3. drowsy	・規定する
4. govern	・勢い
5. approval	・眠くてうとうとした

3 ▶ Video Watching & Script Reading 🔊 Audio 20

Watch the video and fill in the appropriate words in the blanks.

Reporter: "Driver Out." That's what it's called when there's no one in the driver's seat of a truck. Like this one which recently barreled 128 kilometers from Tucson to Phoenix, Arizona. Fully autonomous trucks will probably be on
5 the road well before people routinely **1.**_____ **2.**_____ self-driving cars, experts say.

Cheng Lu: Because it's point to point, that's repeater routes, high volume. But this is the really boring drives along the interstates of the U.S.

10 **Reporter:** Autonomous trucking is gaining momentum as the need to move goods around the country increases, and the number of truck drivers decreases, companies say. But not everyone is excited about seeing "driver out" trucks in the lane next to them.

Don Burnette
Kodiak Robotics

15 **Cathy Chase:** We're the ones on the road with these vehicles and the public right now is an unwitting participant in a very highly tech science experiment.

Reporter: There are worries, too, that self-driving trucks will **3.**_____ **4.**_____ some of the more than 3
20 million truck driving jobs in the U.S.

Steve Viscelli: I'd say all drivers are concerned about the future of those jobs. They're not yet convinced of the potential for really upscaling the job.

Reporter: Most of the external sensors in this truck's autonomous
25   driving system are built into the side mirrors, making
    it possible for the truck to **5.**_____ **6.**_____
    7._____ others on the road.

Don Burnette: Our system never gets drowsy, never gets tired, never
    loses attention span. It's always monitoring, many times
30   per second, the world around it. And so we're better
    able to react to situations **8.**_____ **9.**_____
    10._____ the road and handle them in a safe way.

Reporter: While self-driving trucking firms may be itching to hit
    the road, the rules and guidelines governing them will
35   need to win approval first. Michelle Quinn, VOA News.

Notes

ℓ.3 **barrel**「突っ走る」／ *ℓℓ*.3-4 **from Tucson to Phoenix, Arizona** ツーソンとフェニックス
は米国南西部アリゾナ州の都市。／ *ℓℓ*.7-8 **high volume**「大量輸送の」／ *ℓ*.9 **interstate**「（米
国の）州間高速道路」／ *ℓ*.14 **lane**「車線」／ *ℓ*.16 **unwitting**「知らぬうちに」／ *ℓ*.17 **highly
tech (=technical)**「非常に専門的な」／ *ℓ*.23 **upscale**「（規模を）拡大する」／ *ℓ*.28 **Don
Burnette** 2018年に創業した米Kodiak Roboticsの共同設立者兼CEO。Level 4（⇨ p. 75参照）
の自動運転技術の確立を目指す。／ *ℓ*.33 **trucking firm**「運送会社」／ *ℓℓ*.33-34 **hit the road**「出
発する」

Vocabulary Check – 2nd Round ·····················

Choose the appropriate words below to fill in the blanks in the English sentences. Change forms if necessary.

| convince | handle | itch to | monitor | routinely |

1. There were many complaints from the customers but the store manager _____ the problem very well.

2. The cars are _____ tested for safety before leaving the factory.

3. It has been raining for three days and the children are _____ go out and play.

4. The government is trying to _____ the public that nuclear energy is safe.

5. Patients' diets were carefully _____ to make sure that got enough protein.

5 True or False ···

Read the following statements and indicate whether they are true (T) or not (F) along with the reasons. If you cannot determine T or F from the text, indicate NG (not given).

1. The test drive on the video is being carried out on a fixed route on U.S. highways. **(T / F / NG)**

_____

2. The reason why the number of truck drivers is decreasing is that autonomous trucking is taking over drivers' jobs. **(T / F / NG)**

_____

3. Truck drivers believe self-driving trucks will expand their jobs in the future. **(T / F / NG)**

_____

6 Comprehension Check ··

Choose the best answer for each question.

1. What does Cathy Chase criticize about the testing of autonomous trucking?

   a. It costs a lot of money for the truck companies.

   b. Traffic has to be controlled during the test run.

   c. People are involved in the test without knowing it.

2. According to Don Burnette, how are self-driving trucks kept safe?

   a. The system constantly monitors what is happening around the truck.

   b The system is remotely operated while monitoring the camera on the truck.

   c. The system sends alerts if another vehicle approaches the truck while driving.

3. What is required before self-driving trucks can actually be on the road?

   a. Truck owners need to be trained.

   b. Guidelines need to be approved.

   c. New lanes need to be added.

7 Retelling the Story ·······································

Re-tell the story presented in the video clip, including the following five keywords.

self-driving trucks	monitor other vehicles	transporting goods

truck drivers	the rules and guidelines

_____

_____

8 ▸ Your Opinion in Writing ·····································

What other jobs could be replaced by AI in the future? Select one and explain why.

_____

_____

_____

_____

9 ▸ Further Information ····························· 🔊 Audio 21

Read the passage below.

Levels of Automation

Level

0 **Momentary*[1] Driver Assistance**

Driver is fully responsible for driving the vehicle while system provides momentary driving assistance, like warnings*[2] and alerts*[3], or emergency safety interventions*[4].

Level

5 **1** **Driver Assistance**

Driver is fully responsible for driving the vehicle while system provides continuous assistance with either acceleration/breaking OR steering*[5].

Level

2 **Additional Driver Assistance**

10 Driver is fully responsible for driving the vehicle while system provides continuous assistance with both acceleration/breaking AND steering.

Level ③ Conditional Automation

System handles all aspects of driving while driver remains
available to take over driving if system can no longer
operate.

Level ④ High Automation

When engaged*6, system is fully responsible for driving
tasks within limited service areas. A human driver is not
needed to operate the vehicle.

Level ⑤ Full Automation

When engaged, system is fully responsible for driving
tasks under all conditions and on all roadways. A human
driver is not needed to operate the vehicle.

Notes

*1 **momentary** 「瞬間的な、瞬時の」／ *2 **warning** 「警告」／ *3 **alert** 「アラート」差し迫った危険に回避行動をとらせるため、ブザー等で知らせること。／ *4 **intervention** 「（運転への）介入」／ *5 **steering** 「ハンドルの操縦」／ *6 **When engaged** 「運転中」

Vocabulary Checklist

Check the boxes after reviewing the meanings
of the words listed below.

Unit 10
Self-Driving Trucks May Beat Autonomous Cars in Race for Acceptance

☐ autonomous car   ☐ drowsy

☐ routinely   ☐ monitor

☐ momentum   ☐ handle

☐ vehicle   ☐ itch to

☐ unwitting   ☐ govern

☐ convince   ☐ approval

☐ built into

Fighting Food Waste: Technology Tells Restaurants What They Are Throwing Away

▶▶▶

食品ロスや廃棄物による汚染問題に対処するべく、オランダのある企業がAIを使った食品廃棄物モニタリング・システムを開発しました。さて、飲食店などでは具体的にどのような効果が出ているのでしょうか。

1 Video Watching for Gist

Watch the video and pick up five keywords. Guess what the main theme (topic/issue) of the video clip is.

2 Vocabulary Check – 1st Round

Match the following words and phrases with correct Japanese meanings.

1. landfill	・〜を取り付ける
2. outfit	・〜を処分する
3. recur	・持続可能性
4. dispose of	・ごみ処理地
5. sustainability	・繰り返し起こる

3 Video Watching & Script Reading 🔊 Audio 22

Watch the video and fill in the appropriate words in the blanks.

Reporter: As much as 40% of food produced in the U.S. goes uneaten, according to the Natural Resources Defense Council. Most of it ends up in landfills, where it releases massive amounts of methane. To help address this global problem, a Dutch company has developed a food waste monitoring system that uses artificial intelligence to help restaurant chefs identify and measure the amount of food being discarded in their kitchens.

Olaf van der Veen: We outfit the waste bin with a weighing scale underneath and a camera unit 1._____ 2._____. And every time something is disposed of, we take a picture and our AI image recognition algorithms recognize the type of food that is being thrown away.

Reporter: The data is instantly collected and 3._____ 4._____ the dashboard to help chefs see any recurring issues.

Olaf van der Veen: Say you waste ten kilos of tomatoes every Tuesday morning. That's what 5._____ 6._____ you. Say your salad buffet doesn't work very well on Fridays because people are more in craving for comfort foods and thus you throw away a lot of them.

Reporter: That's the 7._____ 8._____ insights chefs can now access to drive down their waste, improve their sustainability and profitability.

Olaf van der Veen: Croissant. There's not a chef in the world that likes to cook for the waste bin.

Vonnie Estes: So what their technology is able to do from a restauranter's point of view is really allow them through artificial intelligence to predict and to make the right amount of food.

Reporter: Restaurants don't buy the machine, but pay a monthly subscription fee for the information the machine collects and shares. Since it launched in 2019, the service has helped about a hundred restaurants in Europe save food waste and money, the company says.

Olaf van der Veen: We saved about two to three hundred-thousand kilos **9.**＿＿＿＿＿＿ **10.**＿＿＿＿＿＿, and that has a value of about 1.2 to 1.8 million dollars... so far.

Reporter: The company plans to expand to markets in the U.S. and hopes one day to eliminate food waste altogether from industrial kitchens. Julie Taboh, VOA News.

📖 Notes

ℓℓ.2-3 **the Natural Resources Defense Council**「自然資源保護協議会」ニューヨーク市に本部を置く国際環境保護団体。／*ℓ*.4 **methane**「メタン」[mé θ eɪn]と発音する／*ℓ*.4 **help address**「取り組む」／*ℓ*.5 **a Dutch company** フードロスを把握、削減するためのAIを活用したシステムを開発するオランダ企業Orbisk／*ℓ*.8 **discard**「～を破棄する」／*ℓ*.9 **waste bin**「ごみ入れ」／*ℓ*.16 **dashboard** 必要最低限の指標をPC等の画面上に整理して表示したもの／*ℓℓ*.21-22 **comfort food** 家庭料理・ソウルフード／*ℓ*.24 **drive down**「（費用を）抑える」／*ℓ*.29 **allow** 人 **to~**「人が～することを可能にする」の意

4 ▶ Vocabulary Check – 2nd Round ·····················

Choose the appropriate words below to fill in the blanks in the English sentences. Change forms if necessary.

| crave | insight | instantly | massive | subscription |

1. You can find a _____ number of skyscrapers in Tokyo.

2. I sometimes _____ for something very sweet such as chocolate.

3. He _____ went to bed since he had overtime work yesterday.

4. I gave my mother a TV _____ since she loves watching movies.

5. These books provide an important _____ into the experiences and attitudes of students who studied abroad.

5 ▶ True or False ·····························

Read the following statements and indicate whether they are true (T) or not (F) along with the reasons. If you cannot determine T or F from the text, indicate NG (not given).

1. The system for monitoring food waste in restaurant was developed by a company in Netherland.   **(T / F / NG)**

_____

2. The AI of the food monitoring system helps to figure out every customer's food preference.   **(T / F / NG)**

_____

3. Restaurants have to make a purchase of food waste monitoring system in order to reduce daily waste.   **(T / F / NG)**

_____

Comprehension Check ·····························

Choose the best answer for each question.

1. What does the uneaten food in the US produce in landfills?

   a. Oxygen

   b. Methane gas

   c. Water

2. How does the AI image system work for the food monitoring system?

   a. AI understands the category of wasted food by capturing image.

   b. AI counts the use of waste bin by recognizing chefs' movement.

   c. AI checks every food labeling and alert the expiry date.

3. What is the final goal of the firm which developed the food waste monitoring system?

   a. To remove all food waste from commercial kitchen

   b. To open up new markets in Asian countries

   c. To increase the number of eco-friendly restaurants

 Retelling the Story ························

Re-tell the story presented in the video clip, including the following five keywords.

| measure | artificial intelligence | appropriate amount of food |

| expand the market | food waste |

_____

_____

8 ▶ Your Opinion in Writing ·····························

Food waste has become a severe issue. What ideas do you have to encourage more restaurants to reduce food waste?

_____

_____

_____

_____

9 ▶ Further Information ····························· 🔊 Audio 23

Read the passage below.

Quick Tips for Reducing Food Waste and Becoming a Food Hero

Here are some easy actions you can take to re-connect to food and what it stands for:

Buy only what you need

5 Plan your meals. Make a shopping list and stick to it, and avoid impulse buys[*1]. Not only will you waste less food, you'll also save money!

Store food wisely

Move older products to the front of your cupboard[*2] or fridge and
10 new ones to the back. Use airtight containers[*3] to keep open food fresh in the fridge and ensure packets are closed to stop insects from getting in.

Love your leftovers

If you don't eat everything you make, freeze it for later or use the leftovers as an ingredient in another meal.

15 ### Support local food producers

By buying local produce, you support family farmers and small businesses in your community. You also help fight pollution by reducing delivery distances for trucks and other vehicles.

Notes

*¹ **impulse buy** 「衝動買い」／ *² **cupboard** 「食器棚」／ *³ **airtight container** 「密閉容器」

Vocabulary Checklist

Unit 11
Fighting Food Waste: Technology Tells Restaurants
What They Are Throwing Away

☐ landfill

☐ massive

☐ help address

☐ discard

☐ outfit

☐ dispose of

☐ instantly

☐ recur

☐ crave

☐ insight

☐ drive down

☐ sustainability

☐ profitability

☐ subscription

☐ launch

Dogs Can Be Trained to Detect Cancer

Medical Detection Dogsといういうイギリスの団体が、尿や呼気、汗などのサンプルから病気の匂いを見つけるようバイオ探知犬を訓練し、生命を脅かす病気と闘う最前線の研究を進めています。しかし、いまだ、科学的な根拠に乏しいという指摘もあるようです。みなさんはどう思いますか？

1 Video Watching for Gist

Watch the video and pick up five keywords. Guess what the main theme (topic/issue) of the video clip is.

2 Vocabulary Check – 1st Round

Match the following words and phrases with correct Japanese meanings.

1. volatile ・尿
2. diagnosis ・感覚的な
3. sensory ・診断
4. frustrating ・揮発性の
5. urine ・イライラする

3 ▶ **Video Watching & Script Reading** 🔊 **Audio 24**

Watch the video and fill in the appropriate words in the blanks.

Narrator: This is where they believe man's best friend might also be his life saver. These dogs or pets are being trained to sniff out prostate cancer.

Rob Harris: See, See.

5 **Narrator:** Kiwi, the Labrador, searches samples of urine. **1.**_____
2._____, she's found the cancer.

Rob Harris: Indication five.

Trainer: Correct.

10 **Rob Harris:** These dogs are being trained to detect the volatile signature for prostate cancer, so what they're using is their incredible sense of smell to analyze all of these chemicals that are **3.**_____ **4.**_____ a urine sample and then they're looking for a pattern that's specific for prostate cancer.

15 **Narrator:** This three-year trial in Milton Keynes will use three thousand samples from real patients. **5.**_____ **6.**_____
7._____ prove how accurately dogs can detect human cancer.

Reporter: To give you an idea how sensitive their noses are, these dogs can detect the equivalent of a drop of blood in two
20 Olympic-sized swimming pools.

Narrator: And that's why they could make a huge difference, because prostate cancer diagnosis is notoriously difficult, involving a blood test, physical examination and a biopsy.

Dr. Claire Guest: The dog is a biosensor. He's actually a highly
25 sophisticated biosensor. He's got 300 million sensory receptors on his nose. He's got a fluffy coat and a waggy tail. That doesn't make the science behind what he's doing any less real. If we can prove the accuracy of these dogs and have a test that's at 90% reliable, then that's the most reliable test

30 currently available in prostate testing.

Narrator: Prostate cancer is the most common form of male cancer affecting one in eight men. The current blood test fails to detect the cancer in 15% of men and gives a false positive in 76% of cases.

35 **Narrator:** Chris Eglington's diagnosis took nearly four months before prostate cancer was confirmed. The long wait made his experience all the more difficult.

Chris Eglington: I was worried. You realize why you're being tested because you ask questions. And **8.**_____ **9.**_____

40 **10.**_____ that magic word or dreadful word 'cancer' is mentioned, you really do feel terrible and I had to go home from the examination and tell my wife and family what the problem was. So it's quite frustrating.

Narrator: Chris welcomes the idea of diagnosis by dog. But at Prostate

45 Cancer UK, they're concerned the science doesn't add up.

Dr Lain Frame: I think that the researchers themselves have problems in identifying what's an aggressive and a non-aggressive cancer by using the dogs. So we know the dogs are detecting something in the urine, but we don't know what it is and so

50 and we don't know whether it's aggressive, or non-aggressive so that in a sense doesn't take us any further forward.

Narrator: But Medical Detection Dogs say the trial will look at differentiating cancers. They hope to work with the NHS and are confident when it comes to prostate cancer detection, the

55 future could well be four-legged. Laura Bundock, Sky News.

📖 **Notes**

ℓ.3 **prostate cancer** 「前立腺がん」 *ℓ*.5 **Labrador (Retriever)** 「ラブラドル・レトリーバー犬」Labとも略す。 *ℓ*.23 **biopsy** 「生体組織検査」 *ℓ*.24 **biosensor** 「人間・動物の身体的な刺激に敏感に反応し、その情報を伝える装置」 *ℓ*.26 **receptor** 「（生化学用語で）受容体」 *ℓ*.26 **waggy** 「揺れやすい」 *ℓ*.45 **add up** 「知見が蓄積される」 *ℓ*.47 **aggressive** 「（医学用語で）進行の早い、悪性の」 *ℓ*.53 **NHS** National Health Serviceという英国の健康保険制度、または、その制度の提供を受けている病院。 *ℓ*.55 **four-legged** 「四足の動物」

Vocabulary Check – 2nd Round ·····················

Choose the appropriate words below to fill in the blanks in the English sentences. Change forms if necessary.

| analyze | differentiate | dreadful | involve | sophisticated |

1. Researchers _____ surveys returned by approximately 300 participants last year.

2. There was very little scientific research _____ .

3. He was a _____ writer of mystery novel.

4. He can easily _____ varieties of insects since he loves them.

5. Yesterday's weather was so _____ that I could not go out.

5 ► True or False ···

Read the following statements and indicate whether they are true (T) or not (F) along with the reasons. If you cannot determine T or F from the text, indicate NG (not given).

1. Dogs can identify different types of chemicals by sniffing.　　　**(T / F / NG)**

_____

2. The current testing for prostate cancer has already achieved 90% reliability.

(T / F / NG)

_____

3. Costs for training cancer detection dogs is one of the biggest concerns.

(T / F / NG)

_____

Comprehension Check ·····························

Choose the best answer for each question.

1. Why are "a drop of blood" and "two olympic sized pool" mentioned in this passage?

 a. To show the difficulty of blood test

 b. To indicate how sensitive dogs' noses are

 c. To illustrate the process of prostate testing

2. How accurate is the current blood testing for detecting prostate cancer?

 a. It gives wrong results in 76% of cases.

 b. It misses 30% of male prostate cancer.

 c. It has not shown the accuracy rate yet.

3. Why does Dr. Lain Frame say cancer-detecting dogs cannot go further?

 a. Because dogs cannot identify cancer as aggressive or non-aggressive.

 b. Because many scientists in the UK disagree with using dogs.

 c. Because cancer-detecting dogs have an issue with animal protection.

 ## Retelling the Story ······························

Re-tell the story presented in the video clip, including the following five keywords.

| train to identify | analyze chemicals | prostate cancer | reliable test |

| aggressive and non-aggressive cancers |

Your Opinion in Writing ·······································

Do you think that training dogs for finding cancer is a good idea? Please explain your opinion with reasons.

_____

_____

_____

_____

 Further Information ······························· **Audio 25**

Read the passage below.

Sniffer[1] Dog Cancer Tests Yield Results
But Require Trainers, Funds

In Japan, there are only five cancer sniffer dogs. All of them were trained by Yuji Sato, 70, who heads a dog training center, St. Sugar Japan, based in Tateyama, Chiba Prefecture, near Tokyo.

It costs about 5 million yen ($44,000) to train a dog over three
5　years. To boost effectiveness, two years or more of additional training may be needed, according to Sato. Although Sato is willing to train more dogs or teach handlers[2], he said, "With the current financial capacity, the five dogs are the maximum that I can handle on my own."

10　The screening work, undertaken in a small room, requires intense concentration; each dog works for about 15 minutes every morning and gets a stress release by playing outside in the afternoon.

15　Researchers and doctors say that more donations, corporate investment or financial aid from the state are required for more handlers and dogs to be trained. They say such investments are worthwhile because it enables medical costs to be significantly reduced when cancers are detected early.

 Notes

*1 **sniffer** 「探知する」／ *2 **handler** 「トレーナー」

Vocabulary Checklist

Check the boxes after reviewing the meanings
of the words listed below.

Unit 12
Dogs Can Be Trained to Detect Cancer

- ☐ analyze
- ☐ sniff out
- ☐ incredible
- ☐ analyze
- ☐ specific
- ☐ sensitive
- ☐ diagnosis
- ☐ notoriously

- ☐ sophisticated
- ☐ sensory
- ☐ fluffy
- ☐ accuracy
- ☐ dreadful
- ☐ frustrating
- ☐ in a sense
- ☐ differentiate

100,000 People Have Pledged to Stick to a Plant-based Diet for What's Being Called 'Veganuary'

▶▶▶

"Veganuary"という言葉を知っていますか？ 「ヴィーガン」(Vegan)と「1月」(January)を掛け合わせた言葉で、1月の1ヶ月間ヴィーガン生活を送るキャンペーンなのだそうです。「ヴィーガン」は環境にも優しいと主催者たちは口を揃えますが、これに納得していない意外な業界があります。

 ## Video Watching for Gist ·······

Watch the video and pick up five keywords. Guess what the main theme (topic/issue) of the video clip is.

 ## Vocabulary Check – 1st Round ·······

Match the following words and phrases with correct Japanese meanings.

1. ditch		・栄養物
2. nutrient		・加工する
3. term		・期間
4. iron		・〜を捨てる
5. process		・鉄分

3 Video Watching & Script Reading 🔊 Audio 26

Watch the video and fill in the appropriate words in the blanks.

Reporter: Kebabs and burgers are top of the menu as soul food in Gloucester, but not everything on the fryer is as it seems. All the favorites served here are 100% plant-based, making this the city's first fully vegan takeaway.

5 **Reuben Lawrence:** In the last 18 months, definitely seen people 1._____ 2._____ open towards veganism and towards thinking about what they're putting inside their body. Most of our customers are meat eaters. They may believe it or not and it's they just love the food and they love 10 the change. And one of the most said phrases is just, "light." They don't feel heavy after they eat the food. So that's what's pulling them back in.

Reporter: January marks the start of the seventh veganuary, with hundreds of thousands expected to ditch meat. Nutritionists 15 say although there are benefits, a vegan diet can't provide everything that a human is used to.

Becky Graham: It's down to the individual. And certainly, if you decide 3._____ 4._____ 5._____ meat, you can find the nutrients to replace it. However, looking at 20 following a vegan diet long term, there are certain nutrients that you definitely would be missing out on. So key things like iron, B12, perhaps vitamin D as well, all of those are found in animal products, but not in plant products to the same extent or at **6.**＿＿＿＿＿＿＿ **7.**＿＿＿＿＿＿＿, be honest.

25 **Reporter:** Organizers of veganuary say going vegan is healthier and more environmentally friendly. Unsurprisingly, one industry not convinced is farming. James Small runs a farm in North Somerset and says quality meat should still be part of our diet.

30 **James Small:** What I'm really keen is that when people are **8.**＿＿＿＿＿＿＿ **9.**＿＿＿＿＿＿＿ **10.**＿＿＿＿＿＿＿ those choices not only for themselves but for the families, that they really look closely at what it is they're going to be buying and why they're going to be buying it. What we do see is a lot of vegan food is heavily processed and has been brought from all around the world and in today's climate, where we started to look at climate change, I think actually we need to start looking at what we can produce at home and looking for a good, sensible, healthy and balanced diet, of which I believe red meat and meat proteins play an absolutely essential role.

Reporter: Sticking with meat or cutting it out completely. Awareness of what we eat and where it's come from is higher than ever before. Dan Whitehead, Sky News.

Notes

ℓ.1 **Kebab**「ケバブ」西アジアや北アフリカの、肉と野菜の串焼き料理。／*ℓ*.2 **Gloucester** イングランド南西部の街。発音に注意 [glɑ́(ː)stər|glɔ̀s-]。／*ℓ*.4 **vegan**「ビーガン」菜食主義者（vegetarian）と違って、卵や乳製品を含む動物由来のものを一切口にしない完全菜食主義者。／*ℓ*.5 **Reuben Lawrence** グロスター初のビーガン料理テイクアウト店 Sowl Fuud のオーナー。／*ℓ*.17 **Becky Graham** 栄養士。／*ℓ*.28 **Somerset** イングランド南西部の州名。チェダーチーズ発祥の地。

4 ▶ Vocabulary Check – 2nd Round ┈┈┈┈┈┈┈┈┈

Choose the appropriate words below to fill in the blanks in the English sentences. Change forms if necessary.

definitely	extent	keen	mark	replace

1. Please do not worry too much, as I will _____ call you when I arrive safely.

2. This year _____ the 200th anniversary of the foundation of our university.

3. You car is in good condition but you ought to _____ the tires.

4. I am not _____ on going to the concert on my own.

5. We remember the good times and forget the bad to some _____.

5 ▶ True or False ┈┈┈┈┈┈┈┈┈┈┈┈┈┈┈┈┈┈┈┈┈┈┈┈┈

Read the following statements and indicate whether they are true (T) or not (F) along with the reasons. If you cannot determine T or F from the text, indicate NG (not given).

1. Many people will start to avoid eating meat from January. **(T / F / NG)**

_____

2. A nutritionist Becky Graham says a vegan diet contains both benefits and disadvantages. **(T / F / NG)**

_____

3. Even the farming industry is getting to support a vegan diet. **(T / F / NG)**

_____

6 ▶ Comprehension Check ·····································

Choose the best answer for each question.

1. According to Reuben Lawrence, why do people prefer vegan food?

   a. Because vegan food is easily digested

   b. Because more people dislike meat

   c. Because some religions forbid people from eating meat

2. What does nutritionist Becky Graham actually comment on a vegan diet?

   a. It has already helped people spend healthier life in the long term.

   b. It makes people lack certain nutrients found only in animal products.

   c. Its effect on people is still uncertain and therefore more research is necessary.

3. What does a farmer imply in relation to vegan diet?

   a. A lot of vegan food requires special care for transportation.

   b. A lot of meat unpurchased can now be delivered to the developing countries.

   c. A lot of energy is used whatever we produce vegan food or meat.

7 ▶ Retelling the Story ·····································

Re-tell the story presented in the video clip including the following five keywords.

| vegan food/diet | nutrition | farming industry | transported |

| all around the world |

_____

_____

8 ▶ Your Opinion in Writing ·····································

Do you agree with the campaign of veganuary and ditching meat? Why or why not? Write at least six sentences.

_____

_____

_____

_____

9 **Further Information** ···································· 🔊 Audio 27

Read the passage below.

WHO WE ARE AND
HOW WE MAKE A DIFFERENCE

Originating in England, Veganuary is an international organisation that is changing the way we eat by driving a global shift towards plant-based food.

Through the Veganuary campaign, we encourage millions of people to eat vegan in January (and beyond) and work with thousands of businesses around the world to increase their vegan options to capitalize on[*1] this audience. This in turn inspires many more people to try the vegan options that are more easily available. Our huge media presence and strong social media following[*2] further increase the visibility of veganism and the growing plant-based food revolution.

OUR VISION

Our vision is simple; we want a vegan world.

A world without animal farms and slaughterhouses[*3]. A world where food production does not decimate[*4] forests, pollute rivers and oceans, exacerbate[*5] climate change and drive wild animal populations to extinction[*6].

OUR MISSION

Our mission is to inspire and support people to try vegan, drive corporate change[*7], and create a global mass-movement championing[*8] compassionate food choices with the aim of ending animal farming, protecting the planet and improving human health.

This article is reproduced with the kind permission of Veganuary, a charity registered in England and Wales with charity number 1168566.

 Notes

[*1] **capitalize on~**「～から利益を得る」／[*2] **following**（通例、単数形で集合的に）「フォロワー、支持者、ファン」／[*3] **slaughterhouse**「食肉加工工場」／[*4] **decimate**「破壊する」／[*5] **exacerbate**「悪化させる」／[*6] **drive A to B**「AをBに追いやる」／[*7] **corporate change**「企業の変革」／[*8] **championing**「～を支持する」

Vocabulary Checklist

Check the boxes after reviewing the meanings
of the words listed below.

Unit 13
100,000 People Have Pledged to Stick to a Plant-based Diet for What's Being Called 'Veganuary'

- ☐ definitely
- ☐ mark
- ☐ ditch
- ☐ nutrient
- ☐ replace
- ☐ term

- ☐ iron
- ☐ extent
- ☐ unsurprisingly
- ☐ keen
- ☐ process
- ☐ sensible

Artificial Intelligence Cannot Replace Doctors, Can Work Alongside Them

英国のバビロン・ヘルス社が提供しているのは、世界のどこにいてもスマホで健康相談を受けられるAI搭載型アプリ。ユーザーの症状をAIドクターが分析し「診断」までしてくれるといいます。しかしAIドクターではその診断精度が心配だという声もあり、論争が尽きません。

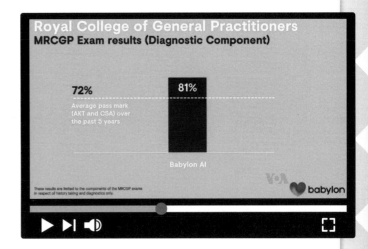

1 Video Watching for Gist

Watch the video and pick up five keywords. Guess what the main theme (topic/issue) of the video clip is.

2 Vocabulary Check – 1st Round

Match the following words and phrases with correct Japanese meanings.

1. accurate	・	初期医療
2. rotate through	・	順に回る
3. primary care	・	正確な
4. clinical	・	登録された
5. registered	・	臨床の

3 Video Watching & Script Reading 🔊 Audio 28

Watch the video and fill in the appropriate words in the blanks.

Louise: Hi, Alexa. I want to speak to Babylon.

Alexa: Hello, Louise. How can I help you?

Louise: Well, I've been feeling a bit dizzy recently.

Reporter: Using Amazon's voice controlled assistant, Alexa, the
5   software created by Babylon Health can interpret symptoms
and tell a person what might be wrong with them after a
series of questions.

Louise: Yeah. Sometimes it feels like the room's spinning.

Ali Parsa: What we're **1.**_____ **2.**_____ **3.**_____
10   **4.**_____ Babylon is make health care accessible,
affordable. Put it in the hands of every human being on Earth.

Ali Parsa: But the question is, how accurate is it? Can it ever, ever
be as accurate as a human doctor in diagnosis?

Reporter: At an event in London, Babylon's founder, Dr. Ali Parsa,
15   says the app **5.**_____ **6.**_____ to replace primary
care doctors also known as general practitioners, but it can
be used to lessen their work. Stanford University Dr. Megan
Mahoney is a believer in the technology.

Megan Mahoney: We do face a shortage of primary care in the
20   United States, and it's been difficult to recruit people into
primary care because they see what it's like. They rotate
through those clinics and they see that there are just 50%
7._____ **8.**_____ time is, is paperwork.

Reporter: But the program will never replicate the level of care
25   offered by humans, says Kamila Hawthorne, **9.**_____
10._____ it has some benefits.

Kamila Hawthorne: But that's all about knowledge and how they
use knowledge, but it's not about clinical skills. It's not about
caring for the patient. It's not about knowing the patient

30 who's come to see you and their family and their community
and the area and the work that they do, which is just so much
richer and so much more important to patients.

Reporter: At Babylon House's London offices, Dr. Mobasher Butt
says the technology allows for an increase in accuracy.

35 **Mobasher Butt:** We've also seen that actually when you look at the
conditions that a GP would see most commonly and actually
waits the results for those most commonly seen conditions,
actually the accuracy of the AI goes up to 96%. And what that
shows is that as the machine continues to learn, there's real
40 opportunity for that accuracy to continue to improve.

Reporter: Since 2016, Babylon has partnered with the Rwandan
government to deliver accessible healthcare via mobile phone
to about two million registered users in rural and remote
areas. Dr. Hawthorne says in those circumstances, the AI
45 technology provides exciting opportunities. Mariama Diallo,
VOA News.

Notes

ℓ.5 **Babylon Health** デジタルでの医療サービス提供をビジネスとするサービスプロバイダー。2013
年に英国で設立。／ *ℓ.17* **Stanford University** 米国カリフォルニア州にある私立大学。／ *ℓ.36*
GP 「総合診察医」general practitionerの略。特に英国では、かかりつけ医として事前に登録され、
不調の場合はまずGPの診察を受ける。

4 ▶ Vocabulary Check – 2nd Round ·····················

Choose the appropriate words below to fill in the blanks in the English sentences. Change forms if necessary.

| affordable | interpret | benefit | replicate | symptoms |

1. Freud is famous for attempting to _____ the meaning of dreams.

2. Common _____ of colds include sore throat and high fever.

3. This is a top-quality property at a very _____ price.

4. The new service will be of great _____ to our customers.

5. This finding is unusual, so need to be _____ before applied for new medicine.

5 ▶ True or False ·····························

Read the following statements and indicate whether they are true (T) or not (F) along with the reasons. If you cannot determine T or F from the text, indicate NG (not given).

1. Babylon Health's software can tell you how to cure your disease.　**(T / F / NG)**

_____

2. Main concern of the new application is how accurate their results are.

(T / F / NG)

_____

3. Dr. Mobasher Butt warns of too much dependence on the AI.　**(T / F / NG)**

_____

6 Comprehension Check ·······················

Choose the best answer for each question.

1. According to the Babylon's founder, what is the purpose of inventing the application?

    a. To help general practitioners increase their skills

    b. To reduce general practitioners' workload

    c. To take the place of general practitioners

2. According to an opponent of introducing the software, what is important for patients?

    a. Clinical skills

    b. How doctors use knowledge

    c. Interaction with patients

3. What has Babylon started in Rwanda?

    a. Collecting more data for the AI to learn a variety of cases

    b. Engaging in experiments to invent the new application

    c. Helping people access healthcare more easily

7 Retelling the Story ····························

Re-tell the story presented in the video clip, including the following five keywords.

software   symptoms   accurate   replace GPs

replicate the level of caring

_____

_____

8 ▶ Your Opinion in Writing ·······························

Would you like to have the Babylon's software check your symptoms? Why or why not? Write at least six sentences.

_____

_____

_____

_____

9 ▶ Further Information ·······························   🔊 Audio 29

Read the passage below.

Babylon Health

Babylon Health is a healthcare provider that provides remote consultation with doctors and healthcare professionals via text and video messages[*1] via a mobile app.

Users can send questions or photos to the company's health
5　care team (including doctors, nurses, and therapists) in a manner similar to a text message. Alternatively, users can video consult a doctor to answer questions about common medical topics such as fever, sore throat, allergies, skin irritations[*2], and colds. The service also allows users to receive referrals[*3] to health
10　professionals, send prescriptions[*4] for medications by e-mail or send them to a pharmacy[*5], or consult therapists to discuss topics such as depression and anxiety. In situations where a physical examination[*6] is required, users can book[*7] health examinations with a limited number of facilities in London. Visits by nurses
15　are limited to one location.

In addition to direct healthcare services, users have access to a variety of health monitoring tools such as an activity tracker[*8], ordering home blood test kits, and viewing general lifestyle and fitness questions.

Notes

[*1] **text and video messages**「文字と動画のメッセージ」／[*2] **skin irritation**「肌の炎症、かゆみ」／[*3] **referral**「紹介」／[*4] **prescription**「処方箋」／[*5] **pharmacy**「調剤薬局」drugstore の中に設置されている場合もある。／[*6] **physical examination**「（カウンセリングだけではなく）実際の検査」／[*7] **book**「予約する」／[*8] **an activity tracker** 心拍数や消費カロリーなど、フィットネス関連の数値を計測・追跡するデバイス。フィットネストラッカーとも呼ばれる。

Vocabulary Checklist

Check the boxes after reviewing the meanings
of the words listed below.

Unit 14
Artificial Intelligence Cannot Replace Doctors, Can Work Alongside Them

☐ benefit

☐ dizzy

☐ interpret

☐ symptoms

☐ affordable

☐ accurate

☐ rotate through

☐ primary care

☐ rotate

☐ replicate

☐ clinical

☐ registered

☐ rural

Above New York, a Giant Green Roof Tries to Reduce Carbon Footprint

ニューヨークの巨大な国際展示場、ジャビッツ・センターの屋上には、外観からはとても想像できない広大な屋上農園が広がっています。この農園は、年間最大約18トンの野菜や果物の生産を目標にしているそうです。

 ## 1 Video Watching for Gist

Watch the video and pick up five keywords. Guess what the main theme (topic/issue) of the video clip is.

2 Vocabulary Check – 1st Round

Match the following words and phrases with correct Japanese meanings.

1. irrigate	・植物
2. vegetation	・流出
3. mitigate	・回復
4. runoff	・（土地に）水を引く
5. resilience	・軽減する

3 ▶ Video Watching & Script Reading 🔊 Audio 30

Watch the video and fill in the appropriate words in the blanks.

Reporter: High atop the Javits Convention Center in New York City lies a nearly 2.8-hectare expanse of vegetation. The 35-year-old convention center is modernizing its rooftop space with plans for a vegetable garden and solar farm.

5   **Jacqueline Tran:** We have a one-acre farm that's operated by Brooklyn Grange, **1.**_____ **2.**_____ **3.**_____ we have an orchard with nearly forty fruit trees.

Reporter: Call it a "Roof to Table" experience. Over 18,000 kilograms of fruits and vegetables are anticipated each year.
10   And they'll be used in the convention halls, kitchens and catering operations. Green roofs like this one don't offset all of the energy used by convention goers below, but demonstrate novel ways to keep buildings cooler in the summer, mitigate urban heat and absorb stormwater runoff.

15   **Jacqueline Tran:** There's two cisterns underground that capture and treat rainwater and pump it **4.**_____ **5.**_____ **6.**_____ the roof to irrigate all of the crops on the farm.

Reporter: In New York City, newly constructed homes and buildings are required to install either solar panels, green roofs or both.
20   Owners get a tax abatement in return as part of the city's larger effort to be carbon neutral by 2050. The Javits Center doesn't qualify for tax abatements because it's a state-run entity.

Timon McPhearson: New York's really made some great strides in
25   providing actual funding to incentivize green roof investments. But it is a **7.**_____ **8.**_____ total compared to our goals, pretty lofty goals, about how we want to advance New York for resilience and sustainability.

Reporter: Solar panels here could supply about 10% of the building's

30　energy needs. Engineers say these rooftop installations could be an important step for reducing reliance on traditional energy sources nationwide.

Matt Helgeson: I mean, if we could do that across the country, we could make a significant impact on our resilience and reliance 35　on the energy grid and just our energy consumption overall.

Reporter: Still, there's no getting around the fact that green roofs are expensive, typically costing over $215 per square meter according to the Green Roof Researchers Alliance. And they require major investment in time as well, monitoring and 40　evaluating how the roof provides benefits over time.

Timon McPhearson: Who pays in the meantime for that actual cost? It makes it very difficult for building owners to want to invest and putting a green roof on their building if they're going to have to pay for all the upfront costs over multiple years.

45　**Reporter:** While the payoff may take time to realize, at least in this 9.＿＿＿＿＿＿ 10.＿＿＿＿＿＿ the city, this route provides a vision of a greener future. Tina Trinh, VOA News, New York.

 Notes

Title **carbon footprint** 商品やサービスの原材料の調達から生産、流通を経て最後に廃棄・リサイクルに至るまでに排出される温室効果ガスの排出量をCO₂に換算したもの。／*ℓ*.1 **Javits Convention Center** ニューヨーク市マンハッタンにある大型の会議などを行う複合施設。／*ℓ*.2 **hectare** 「ヘクタール」面積の単位＝1万平方メートル。／*ℓ*.5 **acre** 「エーカー」面積の単位＝約4047平方メートル。／*ℓℓ*.5-6 **Brooklyn Grange** 5.6エーカーの都市農園で、地元のレストランや市場のために野菜や蜂蜜を栽培している。／*ℓ*.13 **novel** 今までにない、新しい／*ℓ*.15 **cistern** 「貯水槽」／*ℓ*.20 **abatement** 「減額」／*ℓ*.21 **carbon neutral** カーボンニュートラルな、人間が排出する二酸化炭素量を植物の二酸化炭素吸収量などと相殺し、ゼロになっている状態。／*ℓ*.23 **entity** 「団体」／*ℓ*.35 **energy grid** 「エネルギー供給網」／*ℓ*.38 **Green Roof Researchers Alliance** グリーンルーフを研究し、その普及を促進するために21の異なる機関から異なる60名以上の研究者、教育者、政策立案者が参加する共同事業体

4 ▶ Vocabulary Check – 2nd Round ······················

Choose the appropriate words below to fill in the blanks in the English sentences. Change forms if necessary.

| incentivize | lofty | offset | payoff | stride |

1. You do not have to set _____ goals to achieve this.

2. I believe his merits can _____ his demerits.

3. The country has made great _____ in improving public security.

4. The teacher successfully _____ his students to finish assignment last year.

5. I don't think the _____ is worth the effort.

5 ▶ True or False ···································

Read the following statements and indicate whether they are true (T) or not (F) along with the reasons. If you cannot determine T or F from the text, indicate NG (not given).

1. People at the convention halls can have fruits and vegetable grown on top of the buildings.   **(T / F / NG)**

_____

2. In New York City, each new house has to build charging facility for electric vehicles.   **(T / F / NG)**

_____

3. Installing solar panels can contribute only a little to reducing reliance on traditional energy sources.   **(T / F / NG)**

_____

6 Comprehension Check ··

Choose the best answer for each question.

1. What benefit can new home owners obtain by installing solar panels or green rooftops at their new houses?

   a. Social insurance

   b. Electric cars

   c. Tax reduction

2. What would happen if rooftop installations were made available across the country?

   a. The world economy would develop further.

   b. Traditional energy consumption would be reduced significantly.

   c. The country would proactively deal with environmental issues.

3. What is needed to evaluate a green roof?

   a. More time and investment

   b. Financial support from the government

   c. Public awareness of environment

 7 Retelling the Story ···

Re-tell the story presented in the video clip, including the following five keywords.

| **rooftop gardens** | **install** | **become carbon neutral** |

| **responsibility for the cost** | **make the profits** |

8 Your Opinion in Writing ··

Do you think that installing green rooftops is an effective way to make a carbon neutral society? Why or why not? Please explain your opinion with reasons.

_____

_____

_____

_____

9 Further Information ······························· 🔊 Audio 31

Read the passage below.

Greening the Roofs of the World

Green roofs are not a new concept, but of late[1], one that slowly seems to be attracting more and more interest. According to Tree Hugger[2], the popularity of green roofs is growing by 35% in the United States in the past couple of years.

5　Cities around the world are making green roofs mandatory in new building construction. For example, the city of Toronto went as far as making it mandatory[3] that all new buildings be constructed with roof gardens comprising 20-50% of roof space, similar to the Tokyo Green Plan[4] passed in 2001.

10　Germany began developing green roof technology in the 1960s and is today known as the world leader in research and usage with the number of green roofs there increasing 10–15 percent each year. From browsing the international database, one can see the many varieties of green roofs that are being built around the world

15　today.

Notes

*1 of late 「最近の」／***2 Tree Hugger** ニュースや、環境にやさしいデザイン、家、庭などのテーマについて報告する持続可能性のWebメディア。／***3 mandatory** 「義務的な」／***4 Tokyo Green Plan** 「緑の東京計画」水と緑がネットワークされた風格都市・東京を目標に掲げた緑化に対する取り組み。

Vocabulary Checklist

Check the boxes after reviewing the meanings
of the words listed below.

Unit 15
Above New York, a Giant Green Roof Tries to Reduce Carbon Footprint

- ☐ vegetation
- ☐ cater
- ☐ offset
- ☐ mitigate
- ☐ runoff
- ☐ irrigate

- ☐ stride
- ☐ incentivize
- ☐ lofty
- ☐ resilience
- ☐ payoff

Toward a Diverse Society 1:
Learning English through Video

多様な社会を目指して：メディア動画を通して学ぶ英語 1

2023 年 4 月 7 日　初版第 1 刷発行

編著者　　竹内 理／池田真生子／湯浅麻里子／村上正武

発行者　森　信久
発行所　**株式会社　松 柏 社**
〒 102-0072　東京都千代田区飯田橋 1-6-1
TEL　03 (3230) 4813（代表）
FAX　03 (3230) 4857
http://www.shohakusha.com
e-mail: info@shohakusha.com

本文レイアウト・組版　　株式会社インターブックス
装幀　　　　　　　　　小島トシノブ（NONdesign）
印刷・製本　　　　　　シナノ書籍印刷株式会社

略号＝ 782
ISBN 978-4-88198-782-7
Copyright © 2023 by Osamu Takeuchi, Maiko Ikeda, Mariko Yuasa and Masatake Murakami